ESOTERIC CHRISTIANITY

And Mental Therapeutics

With an Essay on
The New Age By William Al-Sharif

By

REV. W. F. EVANS

AUTHOR OF
Mental Cure

First published in 1886

This edition published by Read Books Ltd.
Copyright © 2019 Read Books Ltd.
This book is copyright and may not be
reproduced or copied in any way without
the express permission of the publisher in writing

British Library Cataloguing-in-Publication Data
A catalogue record for this book is available
from the British Library

"We speak wisdom among the perfect: yet a wisdom not of this age, nor of the rulers of this age, which are coming to nought"

— I Cor, ii : 6

THE NEW AGE

An extract from the essay,
The New Age by William Al-Sharif

The 'industrial revolution', the 'Enlightenment Age' and colonialism had strengthened the power of the British Empire. Britain, in the second half of the nineteenth century, was probably the most powerful and influential empire in the world. The power of the empire, accompanied with the processes of modernisation and secularisation, created a new religious and cultural mental space. A 'New age' became part of cultural, religious and romantic imaginaire and represented a new era in which religion and culture would evolve in the favour of the empire and its British subjects. In 1843, The New Age was established in London. It proposed a society 'for the promotion of humanity and abstinence from animal food'. This society would also disseminate 'correct principles on universal peace, [and] health of soul and body'.

Christianity, in the age of the empire and missionary expansion, was influenced by the cultural aspirations for a 'new age'. Christian thinkers began to talk about a new age for 'the Lord' and Christianity. This 'new age' would fulfil biblical prophecies and embody new opportunities and truths for the Christian faith. Rationalist intellectuals imagined a new age for progress and science.

The philosophical and scientific criticism of Christianity, the elaboration of 'holistic' practices and theosophical ideas, the British colonialism of India and romantic Orientalism had all provided an inventive climate for the promotion of spiritualistic ideas. The process of modernisation and secularisation diminished the traditional authority of social and religious structures and shaped the transformation from the idea of destiny to choice and from providence to progress. Yet, there were individuals who opposed the religious hegemony of missionary societies and the hierarchal 'church religion' and sought spirituality in holism, occultism and esotericism. The individualised conquest of spirituality, which later influenced the New Age discourse, was formulated by modernism which invented 'the conception of a unique self and private identity, a unique personality and individuality, which can be expected to generate its own unique vision of the world'.

In the US, the 'New Age' imaginaire represented a new spiritual consciousness of the human self and was transformed by the ideas of Spiritualism, Transcendentalism, New Thought, Theosophy and Millenarianism. People such as Woodbury Melcher Fernald (1813-1873) and Warren Felt Evans (1817-1889) spoke of the coming of 'new age' spirituality. A weekly journal, New Age, was issued in San Francisco in 1865. The foundation of the Theosophical Society in 1875 in New York was significant for articulating theosophical concepts. This Society, which established its international headquarters in India, romanticised the religions of India and declared to challenge dogmatic religious authority and scientific materialism.

Despite the emergence of Christian evangelism and fundamentalism, the first three decades of the twentieth century witnessed numerous attempts by 'spiritual seekers' to create new spiritualities and seek new 'truths' for the 'new age'. Henry Jenkins says that the period between 1910 and 1935 was 'the first new age' and 'the period of emergence'.

PREFACE.

This volume is designed to complete a series of works on the subject of Mental Therapeutics, the publication of which was commenced several years ago, and which was intended to give a view of the subject in its various aspects. It is hoped the book may be found acceptable and useful to those who are interested in the subject of which it treats. It contains a series of twelve lessons or lectures, which the author has given in a private way to a number of persons who were desirous of learning something of the philosophy and practice of the phrenopathic method of cure. In order that the information contained in the lectures might become more generally circulated, and meet the demands for instruction that are made upon the author, they are committed to the press. There is given in the brief compass of the volume a plain presentation of the principles that underlie the practice of the mental system of healing, so that any person of ordinary intelligence, who is moved by a desire to do good, may make a trial of those directions. The author has endeavored to present to the reader every principle which may be viewed as scientifically and experimentally established, and that is of any practical value, and which it may be proper openly to promulgate to the world at large in the present state of the mind of man.

PREFACE.

Much of the teaching contained in the book has long been occult, and has been withheld from the multitude. In the active enquiring state of the mind of man in the present age, the domains of what is called esoteric science have been invaded, and well-nigh conquered. The system of mental science and phrenopathic practice taught in this volume is believed to be identical with the philosophy of the New Testament and with primitive Christianity, not meaning by that term the popular theology. The well of salvation, or system of healing truth, uncovered by Jesus, has not and cannot be drawn dry, but still springs up into and from everlasting life. The difficulty with the world has been the well is deep, and our modern materialistic science has nothing with which to draw up the living water from its obscure depths. The disclosure of the leading doctrines of the spiritual science of antiquity, and the tenets of the ancient mystic brotherhoods, together with the rediscovery of the science of the correspondence of the natural and spiritual worlds, has given us the key that unlocks the deeper mysteries of Christianity. To the sincere and unselfish enquirer after truth is given to know the mysteries of the kingdom of the heavens, that hidden wisdom which was, and still is, concealed from the sensuous multitude, and revealed only to the "perfect" or fully instructed mind. Christianity, like the profound spiritual philosophy of all the Oriental nations, is a revelation to the celestial degree of man's mind, and when that higher region of our triune nature is unevolved into consciousness, and remains latent, its diviner light is concealed from view by the clouds of sense, "and upon the glory there is a defence" or protecting canopy. (Isa. iv : 5.)

PREFACE.

The best way to learn the principles of mental healing and the profound spiritual science on which the phrenopathic practice is based, is to commence the unfolding of our spiritual and deific powers, under the guidance and oversight of some one who has gone over the winding and spiral path leading up to mountain summits and celestial altitudes of experience. The collection of traditional *opinions* that goes under the name of Christian doctrine, on the gradual development of the intuition, or the intellect of the spirit in man, will give place to the *Gnosis*, or absolute interior knowledge and certitude of truth which was denominated faith by Plato, and Jesus, and Paul. By this supreme intelligence only can men be saved in the full sense of the word, and redeemed from sin and disease. This highest knowledge cannot be taught as our children learn arithmetic and the various external sciences, but must be drawn out from the concealed depths of our inner nature. To aid the student of Christian Theosophy to explore the inner realm of truth into which his own spirit opens, is the object of this volume. If it subserves that use in any one of its readers, it will not have been written wholly in vain. Like the preceding volume of the series, it has been written in the interest of self-healing, and to aid the patient, or sufferer from disease, to climb up from that misbelief and error of the understanding, where disease alone can exist, to that higher range of thought and clearer atmosphere of truth where its existence is impossible. Nothing will afford the writer greater pleasure and satisfaction than to learn of cases where it has been thus useful. A large number of

PREFACE.

letters have been received from every part of the country, and some from Europe, from invalids who have carefully read and studied the two preceding volumes of the author, gratefully confessing the benefit received from them. This has been felt to be an ample compensation for the time and labor expended in their preparation. The system of mental healing which is coming into such prominence and attracting so much attention in the world, has arisen, we sincerely believe, in the order of Providence or that intelligent Life which governs the world, and means a higher development, in the near future, of the inner nature of man. It is prophetic of the termination of the reign of matter and sense, and the re-establishment of the dominion of the spirit. As was said at the opening of the first dispensation of Christianity, so in this age of the second coming of the Christ in the revelation of the glory and power of spiritual truth, we can say, "the kingdom of the heavens is at hand."

The fundamental principle of the phrenopathic method of cure is the law of mental sympathy, not using the word in its popular and superficial sense of pity for the afflicted, but in a wider signification to express the influence of our minds upon other minds. Under certain conditions, and in a state of intercommunion of mind with mind, the thoughts, the ideas, the feelings, and all the operations of one mind are transmissible to other minds, and may be reproduced in them without the intervention of the ordinary channels of sensuous communication, but solely through the operation of what we may be allowed to call mental induction — borrowing the term from the science of electricity — or the diffusive tendency of all mental states. All communication of mind with mind takes place, in fact, in harmony with this law, even when it is effected through written signs or spoken words; for unless the two minds come into the same or like states of thought and feeling, they do not understand each other. To fully comprehend what another speaks or writes to us, his mental state, in other words, his ideas and feelings must to some extent be reproduced in us. This law of sympathy seems to extend through the whole domain of nature; and on it, according to Proclus, was based the system of magic, or the ancient occult science. Through the operation of the law of electrical sympathy or induction, it has recently been proved by experiment, that a small battery in a railroad car, running at the rate of thirty miles an hour, may transmit from the top of the moving car an electric influence to the main wire at a distance of several hundred feet, and a message can thus be sent. It has also been proved that two ships on the ocean at a distance of twenty-five miles apart, may thus communicate with each other, and send and receive messages through the operation of the same principle. But in the realm of mind, the law of sympathy or induction has a still higher and wider range of action. In the world of spirit, its influence is as extended as is that of gravitation in the material universe, and in fact, the latter is but the physical expression of the former. As all life is a manifestation of the one Life, the individual spiritual state affects the whole, but in a greater degree those who are in immediate connection with us. All communication of mind with mind, as was said above, whether it be in this world or what we call the next, takes place in harmony with it. The phrenopathic system recognizes this law of mind, and turns it to a practical account. It simply utilizes a principle that has long been known, and aims to discover the laws of its operation, so as to intensify its action in the cure of mental and bodily disease. We have aimed, so far as possible, to divest it of all mystery, and make it like Christianity, an open wisdom for all humanity. The system demands only of its practitioners that, like the ancient spiritual priesthoods, they possess a sound mental, moral, and physical condition.

EAST SALISBURY, MASS.
March 7, 1886.

CONTENTS.

CHAPTER I.
                                                                    PAGE
The Receptive Side of Human Nature, and the True Method of acquiring Spiritual Knowledge, ... 11

CHAPTER II.
Trust as a Saving or Healing Power, ... 22

CHAPTER III.
What is the Fundamental Idea of Disease? And What is it to heal Disease in Ourselves or Others? 35

CHAPTER IV.
The Unchanging I AM in us, or the Divine and True Idea of Man, ... 46

CHAPTER V.
Is Disease a Reality or an Illusion? 56

CHAPTER VI.
The Fall and the Redemption, or the Fundamental Evil in Human Nature, and the Remedy, ... 66

CONTENTS.

CHAPTER VII.

The Glorification of our Humanity, or Full Salvation from Sin and Disease, ... 78

CHAPTER VIII.

The Breath of God in Man, or the True Elixir of Life, . . . 91

CHAPTER IX.

Pain and its Mental Conquest, ... 107

CHAPTER X.

The Influence of Mind on Mind, or the Doctrine of Mental Spheres and its Practical Application to the Cure of Disease, 120

CHAPTER XI.

Phrenopathy, or Mental Cure, as a Practical System, . . . 136

CHAPTER XII.

The Keys of the Kingdom of the Heavens, or the Power to deliver Ourselves and Others from the Bondage of the Senses, . 158

ESOTERIC CHRISTIANITY AND MENTAL THERAPEUTICS.

CHAPTER I.

THE RECEPTIVE SIDE OF HUMAN NATURE AND THE TRUE METHOD OF ACQUIRING SPIRITUAL KNOWLEDGE.

THE human mind is dual. There is an active, intellectual department of our being, and a passive and receptive nature, and the union of the two constitute the mind. The one is masculine; the other, feminine. This bipartite division extends down through the three discrete degrees of the mind, and even into the body. The function of the one is to act; of the other, to receive and to react. When we turn the receptive and passive intellect towards the realm of light, the "intelligible world," the light of truth will flow in according to our degree of receptivity. In this way, the Hermetic philosophers of all ages and countries claimed to be able to learn all that is known or ever was known; for it all exists in the world of ideas and in the universal Christ, and the Christ within us is in vital communication with it. This turning the receptive side of our mental nature towards the world of light is, in reality, the highest and most effectual form of prayer. The passive soul, with voiceless longing and in tranquil waiting, stands in silence as flowers turn toward the sun to receive its vivifying light and heat. A desire of spiritual knowledge for the sake of some beneficent use constitutes an affinitive attraction for it as certainly as a fading flower attracts the dew of heaven. The mother side of the soul, or the feminine element in man and woman, which is a finite limitation of a universal, formless, receptive principle, is the receptacle and *continent* of all ideas, and from the world of ideas knowledge may flow into it. Thus we acquire knowledge by absorption, as a dry substance in contact with water will imbibe that element and become saturated with it.

Of the universal mother principle, which was one of the most occult doctrines of the Hermetists of all ages, Plato, in the *Timæus*, speaks as " that nature which is the general receptacle of all bodies. For it never departs from its own proper power, but perpetually receives all things; and never contracts any form in any respect similar to any one of the intromitted forms. It lies indeed in subjection to the forming power of every nature, being agitated and figured through the supernally intromitted forms, and through these it exhibits a different appearance at different times. But the forms which enter and depart from this receptacle are the imitations of perpetually true beings, and are figured by them in a manner wonderful and difficult to describe, as we shall afterwards relate. At present, however, it is necessary to consider three sorts of things: one, that which is generated; another, that in which it is generated; and the third, that from which the generated nature derives its similitude. But it is proper to assimilate (or compare) that which receives to a mother; that from whence it receives, to a father; and the nature situated between these, to an offspring."

This receptive nature and absorptive principle is in every one of us. But in receiving knowledge into itself, it must be prepared, or, as Plato says, " it is necessary that the receptacle which is destined to receive all possible forms (or ideas) should itself be destitute of every form (that is, made, as it were, a vacuum). Just as those who are about to prepare sweet-smelling unguents, so dispose a certain humid matter, as the subject of the ensuing odor, that it may possess no peculiar smell of its own; and as those who wish to impress certain figures in a soft and yielding substance (as a wax tablet) are careful that it may not appear impressed with any previous figure, but render it as much as possible exquisitely smooth. In the same manner, it is necessary that the subject which is so often destined to receive in a beautiful manner, through the whole of itself, resemblances of eternal beings (or ideas) should be naturally destitute of all that which it receives." It then becomes a formless universal recipient. (*Works of Plato*, translated by Thomas Taylor, pp. 487, 488.)

Such is the recipient capacity of the soul. The person who has thus learned to imbibe knowledge from its inexhaustible fountain and repository is no longer like the man who has to carry his empty bucket to fill it from his neighbor's well, but has in himself a well of the living water of truth springing up into everlasting life. He has given up the vain and restless search abroad for what he can only find within. He has learned that heaven opens inward. Spiritual truth does not come to us from without; but from the infinite inner depths of our own being which are in communication with the universal Christ, in whom are hid all the treasures of wisdom and knowledge. (Col. ii: 3.)

There is one-half of our dual nature, the feminine moiety in man and woman, that is, in its absorptive capacity, a boundless and passive receptivity, which, when turned towards the ever-present realm of pure intellectual light, receives it into itself; and the union gives birth in us to ideas which are flowers from the garden of God made up of celestial light and dew.

All true education is a spiritual development. Spiritual knowledge is imparted, not by verbal discourse merely, but by the silent influence of mind upon mind. It is a principle that has always been recognized in the world, that one mind, by the influence of its silent sphere, can lift another mind to a higher intellectual level. This is a truth taught by Plato. Sokrates, in his dialogue with Theages (a word which signifies Divine Guidance), tells this story of Aristides, in illustration of the silent communication of knowledge from one mind to another. "I will tell you, Sokrates," says Aristides, "a thing incredible, but nevertheless true. I made a great proficiency when I associated with you, even if I was only in the same house, though not in the same room; but more so when I was in the same room; and much more *when I looked at* you. But I made by far the greatest proficiency when I sat near you and *touched* you."

This has always been a method of instruction practised by the Hindu adepts in teaching the neophyte the principles of their occult philosophy. The *chela*, or scholar, is subjected to the psychological influence of the *guru*, or teacher, who aims to impart to him knowledge through the Universal Mind. The disciple waits upon the master in *a spirit of emptiness*, and the intellectual sphere of the teacher's mind fills the vacuum. This is a method of education and of acquiring spiritual knowledge entirely unrecognized in our Western systems of instruction, but has long been known in the Orient, and was practised by Jesus, and belongs to Christianity. The influence of the still living personality of Jesus, when we come into sympathetic (or psychometric) relations with him, is called the Paraclete, or spirit of truth, which was promised, to teach us all things and guide us into all truth. Jesus teaches more in this way than he ever did by verbal discourse. Jesus came into the world that we might have life, and have it in abundance. As some one has said: "The Scriptures teach, and it is woven into the entire structure of the New Testament, that when Jesus Christ came, there was, through and by him, such a giving of life to souls as made all previous giving seem naught." He lays down his life for men; in other words, he imparts his life, intellectual and moral, to us. He, as an incarnation of the universal Christ, came to be a quickening or vivifying spirit, in a degree that no one else ever was; not as being the only one who is an example of the blending of the life of God with the life of man, but as depositing his own life in his disciples, and *that life was his life as he was after the resurrection and ascension.* The religion of Jesus Christ stands apart from all other religions, and has as its characteristic and distinguishing feature that he can and does lodge himself, and incorporate and repeat himself, in his true disciples; so that they no longer live a mere natural life, but a supernatural life, a life so little their own that Paul could affirm in truth: "I am crucified with Christ: nevertheless I live; yet not I, but the Christ liveth in me." (Gal. ii: 20.)

Through Jesus we come into communication with the Christ, in whom are hid all the treasures of wisdom and knowledge. The best schooling we can get in the principles of esoteric Christianity is an hour's communion every day with Jesus. We may in this way not only imbibe the light of the higher world, but its life also. Through Jesus, as a mediating personage, we may come into a living communication with the universal and only saving principle, which his name signifies and represents. Just as if we were in the foul, poisonous air of a dungeon, and a tube should be let down, communicating with the upper and purer air — the air of immensity. Through this we can breathe the breath of life, the pure air of the boundless heavens. So in Jesus we have a communication with the Christ realm, and with the only saving, healing principle.

But Jesus is not a mere external and historic person, but an everywhere present saving principle, which, as being universal, or a one thing which is in all things, is in us. It is, in fact, the principle or faculty of Intuition, the passive and feminine intellect; and the development of this is the first step towards the attainment of spiritual life and knowledge. It is not good for the man in us to be alone. The rational intellect by itself is insufficient. Hence, God is represented as saying, I will make him a help, or a governing or ruling principle (as the word may mean) meet for him, or, as more literally rendered, that answers to him.

Intuition is the birth or evolution of the woman in man, that which is highest, and comes next to God. Its development in man is symbolized by the dove coming upon him. Of Jesus it is said, at the time of his entrance upon his Messianic work, at the age of thirty years (a mystic number), that the heavens were opened unto him, and he saw the Spirit of God descending and coming upon him in the form or quality of a dove, the Hermetic representative of the receptive feminine intellect, the Intuition. (Matt. iii : 16, 17.) It is man's highest guide to truth either in earth or heaven. It is the only faculty in man through which divine revelation comes, or ever has come. By means of it we gain access to an interior and permanent region of knowledge, where are stored up all the truths which were ever known or can be known, — the universal Christ, in whom are hid all the treasures of wisdom and knowledge. By Swedenborg it was improperly called perception. By it we attain to righteousness or a divine rectitude of thought and certitude of truth. For it is the ineffable Word, the voice of God in man. The expression in the Old Testament, —

"I said, Ye are gods,
And all of you sons of the Most High,"

and which Jesus approves in its application to the spirit of man, has a peculiar significance in this connection. It has ever been a doctrine of the esoteric philosophy and religion of all ages and nations, that each immortal spirit is a direct emanation from the "Unknown God," a personal limitation of the Universal Spirit, who is the father of all spirits, as the ocean is of all the drops that compose it. Each individual spirit is not God, but *a* god, and is possessed of all the attributes of its parent source, among which are omniscience and omnipotence. The spirit of man from its inseparable connection with God is possessed of a godlike wisdom, and has deific powers. As Paul has said, when his words are correctly rendered (as John Locke long ago showed), "Without controversy, great is the mystery of godliness which has been manifested in the flesh, justified in the spirit, seen by angels, preached among the nations, believed on in the world, and received up in glory." (1 Tim. iii : 16.)

In seeking for spiritual knowledge we are to look only within. "Man's true good," as Henry James remarks, "never comes from without him, but only from the depths of Divinity within him." The true *organon* or method of acquiring transcendental truth, is that mode of the mind's action termed the intuition. Following this supreme light of the spirit, and turning the mind inward upon itself towards its divine centre, man comes into such relations with his own immortal Self, the *anima divina*, as to be able to receive from that source the knowledges of things that belong to the realm of pure intelligence, and of truths which the higher soul was supposed by Plato to have acquired before her incarnation or descent into matter. By giving this prominence to the intuition, we would not imply any disparagement of the rational intellect, for it is only through this latter that the truths of the intuition can be reproduced and expressed in language. The intellect must be developed and cultivated to the utmost, not as the instrument of discovering, but of communicating truth. Perfecting and combining these two departments of our being, the rational intellect and the spirit, which is the union of the masculine and feminine in man, he attains to the highest knowledge which it is possible for the human mind in this world to reach; for man thus knows God, and to know God is to have and to be God, and " the gift of God is eternal life." (*The Virgin of the World, of Hermes Trismegistus*, p. 15.)

In the progress of our spiritual development we may reach a point where we need no external teacher, "for the anointing that you have received abideth in you, and you have no need that any man teach you, for the anointing (or overshadowing of the spirit) teacheth you concerning all things, for it is the spirit of truth itself." (1 John ii: 27.) The Universal Spirit bears witness with our spirit that we are sons of God, and if sons, then heirs; heirs of God and joint-heirs with the Christ, in whom are hid all the treasures of wisdom and knowledge. (Rom. viii: 16, 17.) The spirit of man searches out all things; yea, the deep things of God. It is the spring of all inspiration and revelation. (1 Cor. ii: 9–16.) As our individual spirit has a voice, so has the Universal Spirit, in whom we are included. Let us turn the inward ear towards the " speaking silence " to receive the soundless word, " the deep and calm revealing." If with a sincere desire to know the truth, and live the truth, and use it for the good of mankind, and not from a mere idle curiosity or for the sake of gain, we are found listening at the door of the temple of wisdom and the " halls of learning," the door will be unlocked and thrown open to us, and we may enter in and read the records of the hidden wisdom, which God appointed before the ages for our glorification. It is only in the deep silence of the soul that God speaks. Silence is the bosom of the Infinite Life, and contains the indelible record of all the truth that ever entered the mind of man.

"Silence is the heart of all things; sound the fluttering of its pulse,
Which the fever and the spasm of the universe convulse.
Every sound that breaks the silence only makes it more profound,
Like a crash of deafening thunder in the sweet, blue stillness drowned;
Let thy soul walk softly in thee, as a saint in heaven unshod,
For to be alone with silence, is to be alone with God."

(*Beyond the Sunrise*, p. 80.)

It is not in the noise and bustle of the city with its tainted moral atmosphere, nor in the marts of trade with their sphere of falsehood and selfishness, that spiritual truth is best learned; but rather in the solitude of mountain summits and the deep stillness of primeval forests, where we are alone with nature and with God. The prophets and sages of all nations have known and taught this. To gain the truth, they turned the receptive side of their dual nature towards the world of pure intelligence, and placed a listening ear close to the lips of the living, speaking silence to receive the inner word. Instruction from others may prepare the way for this, but can never be a substitute for it. All the deepest experiences of the human mind tend to silence. There are desires that cannot be uttered (or worded). (Rom. viii: 26.) There is an ecstasy of love that seals the lips; a rapt devotional frame that is dumb; an inward craving for truth, and gravitation of the soul toward it, that can find no words to express it, but turns the soul toward God like the flower toward the sun. Says that little gem of a book, *Light on the Path*, "In time you will need no teacher. For as the individual has voice, so has that in which the individual exists. Life itself has speech and is never silent. And its utterance is not, as you who are deaf may suppose, a cry: it is a song. Learn from it that you are a part of the harmony; learn from it to obey the laws of the harmony." When the outward senses are conquered and their reign broken, and the inner senses are opened, as will be the case in time, we can wrest from all the objects of nature their hidden secrets. The world becomes a book on which is written the history of man. When the outer senses are subdued, and made subservient to the perceptions of the celestial man or mind, we may ask for the lessons of wisdom which the "inhabitants of Zion," the spirits of just men made perfect, or the spiritually enlightened of this world and the world above have to impart to us. For the truly regenerate man is in hailing nearness to the celestial realms, and in sympathetic and receptive *rapport* with all enlightened mind in the world. But above all, let us turn the mind inward toward the secret place of the Most High, or the Divine Iumost, to receive the secret of the Lord which is given to them that reverentially adore him. (Ps. xxv:14.) The highest truths of religion and philosophy are received only by an inward revelation; in other words, by intuition. The lesser mysteries may be communicated by instruction, which is only the interpretation of sacred symbols. The greater mysteries, or spiritual truths, can be received only by the "still small voice" within, which is the "Word of the Lord," the manifestation of the Logos, that came to the prophets, and still comes to men. The secret doctrines of the Jews, which are essentially the same as the "hidden wisdom" of the Hindus, the Egyptians, and the Chaldeans, were called the Kabala, which means *reception*, because they are truths received by an inward revelation, or unveiling, as the word means, of what is already in the inmost degree of the mind. It is an *apocalypse*, or uncovering, of the hidden treasures of man's inmost being. The Masora and the Talmud are only traditional instruction handed down from generation to generation; in other words, it is only public opinion, an uncertain and unsafe guide, and which, when crystallized into a permanent form, is called the *law*. The higher wisdom which comes only from the Christ within is called *grace*. In our search for the hidden wisdom let us study the case of Elijah at Horeb, who represents to us the method of acquiring spiritual truth practised by the greater Hebrew prophets. When the great wind rent the mountain and broke the rocks in pieces before Elijah, he could not see God in the wind, nor in the earthquake which followed the wind, nor in the fire that followed the earthquake. These were only *effects* of the divine presence in nature. But after the fire there came a "still small voice"; and when the prophet heard that, he wrapped his face in his mantle and went to the mouth of the cave, and in "a speechless awe that dares not move," stood before the Lord to receive in silence the inner word. (1 Kings xix : 11-13.) It is only in this "sound of gentle stillness" that the Most High (or Divine Inmost) utters his voice in the soundless and ineffable Word, the inward Logos, the true light that lighteth every man that cometh into the world.

> "So to the calmly gathered thought
> The innermost of truth is taught."

A true faith stands before Jehovah — who is represented on earth by Jesus — in the deep silence of an adoring love, and holds out its empty hand to receive the life and light he is more than willing to give. From within outward, and from the higher region of our mental nature to the lower, expresses the law and order of spiritual development.

> "Why idly seek from outward things
> The answer inward silence brings?
> Why stretch beyond our proper sphere
> And age for that which lies so near?
> Why climb the far-off hills with pain
> A nearer view of heaven to gain?"

CHAPTER II.

TRUST AS A SAVING OR HEALING POWER.

It is said by Jesus, that "the Son (or the individual spirit and soul of man) can of himself do nothing, except what he seeth the Father doing." (John v: 19, 20.) The universal Christ principle, the first emanation from the "Unknown" is the supreme saving and healing power. It is the manifested God. In his (or its) relation to the Supreme Divine Essence, he is the first begotten and only begotten Son. In his relation to us and to all below him, he is the Father, for all manifested life is in him, and goes forth from him. Its characteristic property is an irrepressible tendency to impart itself, and like heat and light which symbolize it in the world of nature, to radiate itself. In curing others, we can only execute the function of mediators between this universal principle and the diseased and unhappy ones to whom we minister. Through us, as a channel of communication, it may come into them. We can do nothing better than this to heal the souls and bodies of men. An undeviating and trustful conformity to the operation of this principle in the world of nature and mind is the highest law of health. The individual and creaturely will must be surrendered to and be merged in the universal will. For the will is the principle of conjunction, and that by which we come into oneness with the Father. Two persons who will in opposite directions are not and cannot be one. Willing in the same direction, they become, as it were, one life in two personalities.

On the subject of trust, the Christian Hindu, Mozoomdar, very truly says: "Trust, as a faculty of the soul, passes almost without recognition. Yet, in spiritual life, it is a cardinal, vital power. It is not a mere feeling. Though its relation to all warmth of sentiment be very deep, it is a positive organ of strength." (*Oriental Christ*, p. 141.) Blessed is the man who has risen from the life of sense, through the life of faith, to the life of trust. Trust is the opposite of fear, which is the fertile root of most diseases.

It is a truth, and a great truth, that there is a divine saving principle, a universally diffused, and consequently ever accessible intelligent and loving Life, that exhibits an endeavor to impart itself and its saving blessedness to everything that breathes. This universal saving principle (or Divine Personage, if we prefer thus to conceive it) lies beyond the apprehension of the senses, and consequently must be perceived and appropriated by *faith*, and taken up into our individual being by *real* prayer; not the noisy supplications that clamorous lips pour forth, but a passive attitude of the mind. It comes to seek and save that which is lost, or to restore to man all that has dropped out of his existence and which is necessary to the realization of the divine idea in him. It is represented and signified by the *name* of Jesus. It is a principle (and in thought becomes limited in a personality) of pure spiritual intelligence, united to its correlative, pure love, which in conjunction constitute it a living substance and force. If we will assume towards it, or him, an attitude of passive trust, it will save us. But how am I to do this? Suppose I desired and needed to warm myself by the light of the sun, how could I do so? The process is simple. I should expose myself to the light and heat of the sun and *let* it warm me. I should make no effort to cause it to shine, but simply hold myself passively exposed to its vivifying rays. This is the only effort of will that is necessary. If there was any obstruction, any opaque substance, between me and the sun, I should remove it. I should take away every screen which could obscure the sun's rays; and then it would shine upon me and penetrate me with its living warmth, even without my asking or entreating it to do so, but by simply trusting it in silence.

This universal saving principle is the same as the τὸ ἄγαθον of Plato, the supreme and eternal Goodness, the Christ of Paul, "a divine human principle" and person. As it is not only good, but goodness itself, it can do to and for us nothing contrary to its nature. We are to trust in it, as an infant reposes on the bosom of the maternal love. An infant's life is bound up in the life of the mother. So our true being is included in this principle represented by the *name* of Jesus. It has an affinity for all sinful and diseased humanity. It not only can be prevailed upon to save us, but it yearns to save. We need only to hold the soul passively open and upward to imbibe its life.

In our efforts to cure others by the mental and spiritual method, we are to identify ourselves with it, and consecrate ourselves to its use, as an organ of communication between it and the patient. Even though we may not speak ourselves the word of life, we can be the silent telephonic wire, through which the vivifying inner word may be spoken to a patient.

This only saving, healing principle in the universe is identical with the *sun* of the spiritual world, as described by Swedenborg, and which he defines as the proximate emanation from the "invisible God." It is the Kabalistic sun of righteousness (or spiritual truth) which arises in our souls with healing in its wings (or elevating power). (Malachi iv: 2.) Its light is the highest intelligence that can come to men, and its heat is a celestial love; and the two in conjunction, and set over against each other in the mystic balance, make it pure life, a divinely vivific principle. (See my *Divine Law of Cure*, pp. 58–60.)

On the reception of this saving influence by assuming

toward it an attitude of passive trust, I said in my *Celestial Dawn*, published twenty-three years ago, "Let us behold this great truth, this divine *arcanum*, or heavenly mystery, in an outward symbol addressed to sense. One of the greatest works of ancient Egypt, surpassing even the pyramids, was the Lake of Mœris, an artificial excavation four hundred and fifty miles in circumference, and three hundred feet in depth, and designed to receive the sacred waters of the Nile, to be used in fertilizing the surrounding lands. Between it and the river there was an obstructing barrier of earth, which was opened by a channel cut through it. Then the waters flowed of their own accord, and by a law of their nature, into the lake and filled it to its utmost capacity. Now the Nile — and the same is true of all rivers — mystically represented the Divinity, and was a symbol of an emanative principle and influence, a *rema*, as it is called in the Scriptures, a flowing forth from the Deity. In the Hindu religious symbolism rivers had the same significance and sacred character. The Lake of Mœris represents the human soul, made to be a recipient of the divine nature and life." So in esoteric Judaism, rivers were sacred symbols. Says the Psalmist, "There is a river (an emanative principle of pure intelligence and life) the streams whereof (or that go forth from it) shall make glad the city of God, the holy place of the tabernacles of the Most High." (Psalm xlvi : 4.) And this river, which represents and signifies the outflowing of the divine love and wisdom, is always full of the water of life (Psalm lxv : 9) ; and when every barrier is removed, and we hold the soul passively and unresistingly open to receive, it will flow in and fill the finite spirit with its illuminating and saving influx.

Jesus, as we have before said, represents the only saving principle in the universe. This is a truth of which we should never lose sight. In the lower manifestation of this intelligent principle in nature, it does the best, whatsoever that may be, for the plant, the tree, the animal, and the man. But there is a higher exhibition of its operation in the realm of mind. Jesus, as an individualized expression of the universal saving principle, and as an historic personage, was an ultimate manifestation of the principle of health, in the full sense of the term. He was perfectly well in soul and body, and a sympathetic conjunction with him brings us into *rapport* with the infinite fountain of health and well of salvation. But Jesus Christ comes in the flesh, or descends to an ultimate manifestation in us. He who believes this is born of God, that is, a divine life is engendered even in his bodily organism. I am not merely to believe in his coming to the world as an event of history (for that faith has only a trifling saving value and efficacy), but that he still comes in the flesh, and in my flesh. (2 John v : 7.) His coming is not a movement through space, but signifies communication by influx. (*Arcana Celestia*, 5249.) By this coming of the Lord to us in the flesh, our external humanity is made divine.

In treating a patient by the method of trust, we should approach him in the *name* of Jesus, that is, we should identify ourselves with the saving principle, which he represents, and through which he can be ever present with us, and in tranquil silence let him speak the *Word*, that saving inner Word, by which he healed, and still heals, the souls and bodies of men. The Divinity still speaks in man, as certainly as he ever did, but in our spiritual deafness and obtuseness, we mistake his voice in us, as did the youthful prophet Samuel. When the young neophyte came to the aged prophet Eli, under the mistake that it was a human voice that called him, he was sent back with instruction to listen to the inner Word, the sacred and soundless speech which God utters in the solitude and silence of our own spirit. The coming of the secret Logos, the inner voice, is the most important event in our life. There are external books enough in the world, both sacred and profane, and of the making of them there is no end; but no one of them, nor all of them condensed into one, is of so much value in our spiritual development as the inner Word. When this speaks, all other books and voices should be silent. In the language of Mrs. Browning: —

> "Hearken, hearken!
> God speaketh in thy soul,
> Saying, O thou that movest
> With feeble steps across this earth of mine,
> To break beside the fount thy golden bowl
> And spill its purple wine —
> Look up to heaven and see how like a scroll
> My right hand hath thine immortality
> In an eternal grasping."

This living Word is, as it is called in the New Testament, a *rema*, a flowing forth, an efflux or emanation from the manifested God, a divine proceeding and proceeding divine. It will come to every one who will assume toward it an attitude of listening and obedience expressed by the words, "Speak, Lord, for thy servant heareth." There is more saving virtue in it than in every remedy known to medical science. "He sent forth his Word and healed them." (Ps. cvii : 20.) This Word is the divine Truth proceeding from the Lord. It was, and still is, made flesh and dwells ἐν ἡμῖν, *in us* (not among us, as if it was something outside of us), and we behold its glory, a glory as of the only begotten of the Father, full of grace (or secret wisdom) and truth. (John i : 14.) This is not historic, but descriptive of what may be a present experience of the soul. We need to be raised out of the historical sense of the Scriptures into the living spiritual sense. The Bible (and the same is true of all sacred books) is not a history of events outside of our minds, like the books of Herodotus and Tacitus, but is a history of every soul, and of the universal soul. It is the inside annals of man.

The inward Word in us is a manifestation of the creative Logos or Word of the Lord by which the heavens were made. (Ps. xxxiii: 6. 2 Pet. iii: 5.) The visible universe is only the outward expression of the Logos, the externalization of the Word. So the inner Word in us seeks and endeavors to come in the flesh, or to manifest itself in a bodily organism in harmony with it. Matter is in itself not evil. In its reality and inmost essence it is divine — the second emanative principle from God. It is only when matter has dominion over spirit, that it is evil. It then usurps the place of God and is idolatry. Matter as it is in itself, and in its place, is *an invisible, divine, and immortal substance*. It is the correlative of spirit — a manifestation of spirit. What we call matter is not matter, but is unreal and an illusion.

There is a tradition that Jesus was asked, "When the kingdom of God should come?" and he answered, "When two become as one, and that which is without becomes as that which is within." This might seem at first sight to express an impossibility, that two should become as one. According to the Pythagorean symbolic numerals, one is spirit and two is matter. And the kingdom of God comes in us, and with saving power, when spirit and matter are no longer at war, but become one *substance*, and the phenomenal is absorbed into the real. The within, the spirit, is the invisible Reality; the without, the body, is the illusory Visible. (*The Perfect Way*, p. 327.) The *apotheosis* of matter, and the glorification of the body, is the highest triumph of faith. This was effected in Jesus, who has gone before us to prepare the way for us, and to open a pathway of light conducting by an unerring straight line to the highest unfoldment of the divine element in man. His life was a life of trust that brought him into such close relations with the Godhead, and indissoluble union with the Father, as to raise his humanity entirely above the plane of sensuous illusion, and the evils that grow with more than tropical vigor in such a soil. Let us follow the path he has marked out for us. In the life of trust millions of souls have found rest, and this "so great cloud of witnesses" still speak to us in the language of David, in one of the most beautiful and expressive sacred hymns of any age or nation: "I had fainted unless I had believed to see the goodness of Jehovah in the land of the living. Wait on Jehovah: be of good courage, and he shall strengthen thine heart: wait, I say, on Jehovah." (Ps. xxvii: 13, 14.)

By trust we rise above the delusion which is natural to the psychical man or mind, that our life is self-originated, instead of being perpetually derived from the Deity, and we come into union with the manifested God. Sundered from him, life and spiritual health would be as impossible as would the existence of the body without food and air. Man, as to his inner and true self, is but a part, a fraction, of a grand whole. Sundered from the whole, he is incomplete — is as nothing. To unite man and God is the central design of Christianity and of all spiritual religions. The whole, the All, that from which all individual life springs, is the Christ, who is called also the Father, as being the parent source of all existences in earth and heaven. Jesus, as an incarnate expression and manifestation of the Christ, came from the supreme realm of spiritual being, and in him was focused the life of the whole. It was concentered in him, and through him we may come into communication with the whole. Without this mediation and conjunction with the unbroken wholeness of life, we are like a branch severed from the vine, which withers and dies. Conscious union with God is our natural condition, and consequently is health in the fullest sense of the word. Very truly does the author of that profound work, *Natural Law in the Spiritual World*, say: "It is not a strange thing, then, for the soul to find its life in

God. This is its native air. God, as the all-surrounding, all-pervading life of the soul, has been the doctrine of all the deepest thinkers in religion. There is a profound saying of Paul, which defines the relation with almost scientific accuracy: 'Ye are complete in him.' In this is summed up the whole of the Bible anthropology — the completeness of man in God, his incompleteness apart from God." But in our fallen and bewildered state we are saying, in the language of Job: "O that I knew where I might find him, that I might come even unto his seat! Behold, I go forward, but he is not there; and backward, but I cannot perceive him: On the left hand, where he doth work, but I cannot behold him: he hideth himself on the right hand, that I cannot see him." (Job xxiii: 3, 8, 9.) Yet he is as near to us as we are to ourselves, but cannot be discerned by sense.

We never saw the air we breathe, and without which we cannot live on earth. Yet we are in it, and it pervades every part and tissue of our bodies, and its gases form a large proportion of our corporeal structure. Separated from it we die. In a clear day, and beneath the blue dome of the heavens, a man need not institute a search to find the all-pervading atmosphere, for we are in it and are a part of it. Nor need we be constantly *trying* to breathe. If we cease our volitional effort at respiration, and our attempt to impel by the force of will the physiological machinery, our breathing will not be suspended, nor will the vital movements come to a halt. We are so interwoven into the very texture of the Divine Existence that we cannot easily be unraveled. Much of our life is wasted in our futile endeavors to live in and from ourselves, apart from God. If we cease all voluntary effort to breathe, the Divine Life of nature will breathe in us and for us, better than we do ourselves, and we need not exhaust all our energies in trying to breathe the breath of life. Neither do we need to make a constant effort to find God and live in him.

The Collective Man, the universal Divine Humanity, is the Christ, of whom Jesus is an incarnation. All men, as to their real humanity, the essentially human principle in them, are included in the Christ, and are finite limitations of him. To view ourselves as isolated and disconnected fragments of this Divine Humanity — as *disjecta membra*, or scattered and disjointed limbs — is unnatural, and an error and illusion into which the soul has fallen and from which it must be redeemed. Jesus as the Christ, the second Adam, who represents in himself the whole of humanity, came into the world for that very purpose. In him, as a manifestation of the all-inclusive Divine Humanity, and as the "Lord from heaven," every human being has salvation, in the New Testament sense of the word, if he only comes to the intuitive recognition of it, and accepts it. If the Christ, as Paul affirms, is all and in all (Eph. i: 23), then my true life is his life, and will have no separate destiny, and may be safely and securely trusted to him. Underneath us are the everlasting arms.

> "How can I sink with such a prop
>   As the eternal God,
>   Who bears the earth's huge pillars up,
>   And spreads the heavens abroad?"

Our immortal self is enclosed in the life of God. To educate the world up to this grand conception was the errand of Jesus to mankind. The sphere of his life is in a perpetual *conatus*, or effort, to save the world from error and disease. He came into the world that the world through him might have life, in the completed sense of that word. He still lays down his life for men. From the exalted sphere of his being, his influence, or the influx of light and life from him, is gradually dispersing the errors and delusions from the minds of men, which are the cause of our disorder and misery, as the fogs and mists of the earth slowly melt away when the sun is shining above them.

It is affirmed by Swedenborg that in our fallen state we can have communication with the life and light of the supreme heavens only by the mediation of celestial spirits and angels, who receive into themselves the life of the whole, and in conjoining themselves to us connect us with the whole. (*Arcana Celestia*, 5983.) Jesus is all this to us, and more. In him the lost link between the highest and lowest in the manifestation of life is restored. In him the perfect ideal, the archetypal man, has forever become the actual. The exhibition to the world of a perfect humanity in the life of Jesus has taught one lesson which our systems of theology have overlooked. It has demonstrated that sin and disease are no part of man. They are not constituents of human nature, for in Jesus we have a man perfectly pure, and without sin and disease. Hence these are no necessary part of human nature, but are an intrusion, an external accretion. To separate them from our essential self in our conception of ourselves, has a redeeming influence. They are to be viewed as something foreign to man. This is one great lesson that the incarnation has taught. The great error of the world is, that men believe that their sins, their errors, their maladies, are a part of their humanity. But in the perfect life of Jesus there is for all ages to come a sublime demonstration that it is not so. It is an object-lesson on a grand scale that can never again wholly fade from the religious consciousness. Jesus was externally and wholly what we are in the inmost and unevolved degree of our being. By beholding him in this light, may we not be changed into the same image, and thus the disciple become as the master? The intuitive recognition of the truth, that sin and disease are no part of the immortal and real man, is the dawn of our redemption. It loosens the rivet in our chains, and they begin to fall off. In the life of Jesus on earth, brief as it was in a historical point of view, there was a projection of eternity into time, and of the infinite upon the plane of the finite, and the depositing of a new and higher life in humanity, the effects of which can never be lost to man. Somehow his life has become connected with the whole of humanity, and what God hath joined together, let not man by a false way of thinking put asunder. The character of Jesus in its freedom from sin and disease, in its spotless purity and healthfulness, exhibits the possibilities of our own human nature, and is the model idea, the exemplary conception, we are to form of our own inner self. In Jesus the *fraction* of the Whole, the All, which we call the individual man, while remaining forever distinct like a drop of the dew of heaven forever crystalized, ceases to be a mere broken number, and returns to the unity whence it sprang. And he is drawing the world up to God after him. (John xii : 32.) If we are tired out with our vain struggle to save ourselves, let us deliver ourselves up to be saved by him, and by that universal principle which his name represents.

The fall of man, or his gradual descent from the light and blessedness of a spiritual existence, and the entrance of disease and death into the world through sin, or the illusions of sense, is a great fact — a truth of history and of our inner consciousness. But the infinite love and life of God, and his redeeming and saving presence in the world of nature and of mind, is a still greater fact. We live in a world, the deepest reality and only supreme reality of which is spirit, the active presence of God, which is more than a match for sin and disease. Every man's own spirit, owing to its inseparable conjunction with the Universal Spirit, is to him the centre of the universe — the point where our life not merely touches the Divine Life as a tangent comes into proximity to a circle, but where it intersects and interblends with the life of God. By trusting this ever-present saving divine power, the healing process is accelerated in the individual man, and also in the collective race, of which we are a constituent element. God's love, which is an incessant impulse to *give*, to impart good and truth, is a stronger force than sin. The darkest night the world ever saw, and which may have seemed to hold the world in its irresistible embrace, has easily and without resistance yielded to the superior power of the dawning light. So as Paul has affirmed, "Where sin (or the illusions of sense) has abounded, grace (or the celestial wisdom) will abound more exceedingly: that as sin has reigned unto death, even so will grace reign through righteousness (or spiritual illumination) unto eternal life through Jesus Christ our Lord." (Rom. v: 20, 21.) That from which we need to be redeemed is the unnatural bondage to the body and the illusions of the animal soul. Says an intelligent Brahmin, Vamadeva Shastin, in a late number of the *Fortnightly Review*, "To escape from corporeal fetters, out of the endless desert of ignorance and delusion, is the soul's supreme concern." And it is the simple lesson of trust taught in this chapter that there is but one power in the universe which can effect our liberation. This truth is well and forcibly expressed by the prophet Isaiah: "I, even I, am the Lord (Yava), and beside me there is no Savior," or health-giver. (Isa. xliii: 11.) We can neither save ourselves nor others. The only saving principle and healing energy is that which is signified and represented by the *name* of Jesus, and this as the supreme life of angels and men stands forever inclined to save. And the best thing we can possibly do is to *let* it save us.

CHAPTER III.

WHAT IS THE FUNDAMENTAL IDEA OF DISEASE? AND WHAT IS IT TO HEAL DISEASE IN OURSELVES OR OTHERS?

WE lay it down as a fixed principle that there is nothing in the body that has not a prior existence in the mind or the soul. This truth is recognized by Swedenborg in his *Science of Correspondence*, which expresses the relation of material things to spiritual things. He says: "There is not anything in the mind, to which something in the body does not correspond; and this which corresponds may be called the embodying of that." (*True Christian Religion*, 375.) The condition of the body — and the same is true of all matter — is always an effect, of which something in the soul is the cause. There is not a motion, or action, or any conceivable condition of the corporeal organism, that is not due to some antecedent action or state of the mind, by which we mean always the principle of thought.

In case of accidents, or chance occurrences, there is always the relation of cause and effect, for it is inconceivable that a thing should occur without a cause, and all causes are mental. Suppose a splinter is inserted in our flesh by what we call an accident, how it will be asked, was the mind the cause of that, since it occurred without our thinking of it? I answer, that we both *thought* and *willed* what led to it. The body did not place itself in the situation where alone such a wound could be received. If it was the result of an action, such as handling a rough piece of wood, the mind alone was the cause of that act, for surely the body did not move itself. Both the body and the splinter were passive.

The only active cause was the mind. And the same is true of all disease.

The essentially vital organs in the human body are the heart and the lungs, and these have an immediate correspondence with the mind. In fact, the fundamental correspondence between the mind and the body is seen in the correspondence of the heart to the love, or the emotional nature, and of the lungs to the understanding or intellect. The two departments of feeling and intellect constitute the whole mind, and all mental action is included in them. And every change of our feelings or emotions is instantaneously translated into a bodily expression by a change in the action of the heart, and consequently by a modification of the circulation of the blood. But this, if continued for any considerable length of time, must of necessity affect the vital condition of every organ and tissue of the bodily structure.

The lungs in their action respond to the intellect, and their movement is always the exact representation of the state of the intellect. Respiration is the primary movement of the body, and is that on which all other movements depend, and there is an importance attached to it, that few ever stop to consider. Whatever affects the respiration must influence every vital action. Respiration corresponds to the understanding, consequently to the state of thought, and likewise to *faith*, because faith is a state of thought. Every change of thought effects a modification of the action of the lungs (as in the act of listening), consequently of the respiration, and this must of necessity affect all the physiological movements and functions. Hence, an act of faith inaugurates a change in the action of the lungs, which is communicated as an impulse in the direction of health to every part of the body. So, also, fear, and every abnormality of the mind, affect the action of the heart and lungs in the direction of disease, for the movements of the heart and the lungs are primary movements on which all others depend. Hence disease must be considered as the translation into a bodily expression of a prior inharmony of thought and feeling. All disease resolves itself into this in its last analysis. We shall not go far from the mark in our diagnosis of any malady when we pronounce it a case of the *divergence of thought from a divine rectitude* — a deflection of the mind from the real truth.

Thought and feeling make the mind; in other words, the *man*. What we are, and all that we are, is but the gathering up into a personal and human form of all that we have thought and felt. Thought and feeling are never in reality separated. Feeling is thought in its boundless and formless universality and indefiniteness. Like the original chaos, or primal cosmic matter, it is of itself waste and void. Thought is feeling defined and formulated and taking a particular direction. All feeling, whether it be a sensation or emotion, is of itself meaningless. Thought, as an activity of the intellect, gives it meaning and quality and form; in a word, a local habitation and a name. On this philosophical principle, stated by Swedenborg, " that the wisdom (or intellect) is the form of the love or feeling," — and by form is meant not merely shape, but quality, — hang great practical consequences. A patient should be instructed that his feelings in and of themselves have no significance. It is only our way of thinking which makes them mean disease or health. On that pivot our destiny turns.

Thought and existence are absolutely identical and inseparable. To think is to exist; to exist is to think. As thought and existence are one and inseparable, it follows that any change in our way of thinking must, by a necessary law, modify our existence. Hence disease, which is an abnormal mode of existence, in its radical significance, is a wrong way of thinking; or, if you prefer to so call it, a *mis-*

belief. The universal life principle, or ground of our existence, is feeling. But being of itself and standing alone a pure indefiniteness, it is without form and void. It takes form, or, what means the same thing, quality, from thought. Hence it is a principle as fixed as the eternal laws of the mathematics, that as I think, so I am. Thought shapes our whole existence, and, like the helm of the ship, determines our course on the ocean of life.

Disease is a mental inharmony, disquietude, discomfort, dissatisfaction. It is, as the word means, a state of unrest. It is an *unbalanced* mental condition. To get a clear conception of this, it is necessary to remark that the mind of man is dual; that is, each degree of our triune nature is made up of wisdom and love, or intellect and feeling. The inordinate predominance of either department over the other is inharmony; that is, it is a loss of equilibrium. In nervous maladies — and these include a very large fraction of all chronic ailments — there is a great preponderance of the feelings over the intellect in the mental life of invalids. They are all feeling, and the intellect is dormant. This mental inharmony expresses itself in the body. Corresponding to the two departments of our mental nature, intellect and feeling, there are two kinds of cerebral substance, the cineritious and medullary, and two distinct classes of nerves, nerves of motion and those of sensation. In disease, the nerves of sensation become morbidly acute, and the nerves of motion correspondingly weak, with a *disinclination* to motion. Of course, the cure must consist in the restoration of the lost balance. But the bodily condition is only the external expression of the mental inharmony. Hence Swedenborg, in accordance with the law of correspondence, by which all outward things signify and represent internal things, or things of the mind, says that to cure signifies to restore the spiritual life of man; because disease and sickness correspond to the state of man when he declines from the truth to the false, and from good to evil. (*Arcana Celestia*, 9031.) In another work he affirms that healing signifies reformation; that is, re-formation by truth derived from good. (*Apocalypse Explained*, 284.) It is the forming anew of the inward man by the truths of faith. Goods and truths, or states of feeling and thought, are so real that the inward man is nothing but his own goods and truths, and which take on the human form. (*Arcana Celestia*, 10,298.) The imparting spiritual truths to a patient, to take the place of his psychical or sensational illusions and fallacies, forms or re-forms the inward man in the image of the heavenly; that is, of health and harmony. The healing of disease is the creation, or generation, or evolution, of a new man, the spiritual man, the Sanscrit *Manas*. The *psychical* or unspiritual man or mind, with all his phantasies, must be dethroned, his empire of sin (or error of the understanding) must be subverted, and the dominion is to be given to the new and higher man, the Christ within, who must reign until all enemies are put under his feet. As it is expressed by Paul, the Christian philosopher, we are to put away, as concerning our former manner of life, the old man (formed by those appearances of truth which belong to the sensuous or animal range of the mind), and which waxeth corrupt after the lusts or desires of deceit; and we are to be renewed in the spirit of our mind, and put on the new man, which after God is created (by the truths of faith) in righteousness and the holiness of truth. (Eph. iv : 22–24.) In another place he enjoins upon us the putting off the old man (the sensuous mind, the external shell of our true being) with his doings, and the putting on of the new man, which is renewed unto knowledge after the image of him that created him, and in which new man Christ is all, and in all. (Col. iii : 10, 11.) As the body is formed of the food we eat, the water we drink, and the air we breathe, so the new man in Christ is formed of the spiritual truths we imbibe. The material body thus made is mortal, and subject to constant change, to disease, and death; but the new man is immortal, unchanging, and undying, and exempt from disease and unhappiness, by virtue of its inherent immortality. This is the cure of disease to some purpose, and health becomes identical with regeneration.

The fundamental idea of health is integrity or wholeness. And this completeness consists in the perfect balancing of the departments of intellect and feeling, or the masculine and feminine elements in human nature. So long as these are out of due proportion and stand unreconciled, they are the occasion of sorrow, suffering, want, and bondage. This condition is the parentage of evil. But when they are harmoniously blended, and act as one, they generate and bring forth harmony and health. Perfected man is *androgyne;* that is, male and female in one personality. The union of the two in a harmonious synthesis is what is called, in the Kabala, *the house,* as in this passage: "Through *wisdom* is an house builded; and by *understanding* it is established." (Prov. xxiv: 3. *Idra Suta,* sec. 312.) When these two elements are separated, or one is greatly in excess of the other, it is a state of inharmony, an *unbalanced* condition, and this is mental disease. Jesus refers to this when he says, "A house divided against itself shall not stand," — the two conflicting elements mutually destroy each other. This state of antagonism between the two component elements of the mind was represented in the Kabala symbolically, by the union of the man and woman back to back; that is, each looking in a direction opposite to the other, and this was evil. It is not good for man to be alone. For all of truth in us that is not united to its correlative good or emotion comes to nought. And all of good that is not conjoined with truth has not in it the quality of permanency. This is expressed in the occult spiritual science of the Kabala thus: "The male is a mere half body; so also the female." (*Idra Suta*, sec. 718.) "Blessings descend not upon mutilated and defective things, but upon that which is complete — not upon half things." (*Idra Suta*, sec. 723.) "Half things neither subsist in eternity nor receive blessings for eternity." (*Idra Suta*, sec. 724.) This was an idea familiar to Paul, who says: "The woman is not without the man, nor the man without the woman, in the Lord." (1 Cor. xi : 11, 12.) When the two departments of intellect and feeling are perfectly balanced, and there is, as Swedenborg would say, "the marriage of good and truth," it is a condition of perfect mental equilibrium. Health, or wholeness, is represented by the balance, or scales of justice, in a state of equipoise. In all diseases there is a loss of balance. Usually the feelings, either as emotion or sensation, are greatly in the preponderance, and this *hyperæsthesia* is always a state of weakness, and accompanied with a disinclination to motion. The principle here unfolded is one of great practical importance in the treatment of disease by the mental method.

Spirit and matter sustain to each other the relation of male and female; that is, the one is active, the other passive or reactive. When they are joined back to back, to use a Kabalistic figure, or are looking and willing in opposite directions, it is a state of war and mental unrest. When they are joined face to face, or look and will in the same direction, and consequently become a unity, it is a state of peace, harmony, and health. The opposition of the flesh to the reign of the spirit, this schism in human nature, the rending asunder of the higher and the lower degrees, and their coming into antagonism, is the fundamental idea in disease, which is first in the mind, and then by derivation in the body. The flesh — the lower and animal soul with its senses and selfish propensities — warreth against the spirit, and the spirit against the flesh. This is the fall of man, the lapse of the soul, and "the great unhingement of human nature." The spirit, the Kabalistic *Kereth*, the Crown, has the right of dominion, and the union of the two regions of our being; the reconciliation of the two warring extremes by the submission of the lower to the higher, is the true conception of the atonement, or at-one-ment. And this can only be effected by *sacrifice*, the offering up of the lower animal and selfish soul to the spirit. This was signified by the various offerings of the Jewish ritual, the offering of animals to God. This had only a symbolic value and efficacy, and signified the surrender of the *anima bruta*, the animal soul in man, to the *anima divina*, the divine soul or the spirit.

The divergence of the creaturely will, or that of the animal soul and its body, from the will of the celestial man, is the root of our mental and physical maladies. This is the condition of human nature everywhere, and of our human nature. This is what ails us in every disease. How we became so, and why, we need not now stop to ask. It is a fundamental fact in the spiritual science of disease. The restoring of this breach, the healing of this schism, the reconciliation of this contradiction, is the aim of Providence, and should be of medical philosophy. If the lower animal soul surrenders to the divine spirit in us, the battle is ended, and peace is declared through the whole mental and physiological domain. As Jesus said, "If any man will save his soul (or tenaciously adheres to the life of sense), he shall lose it. But if any man will lay down his soul for my sake and the Gospel, he shall save it. (Luke ix: 24.) If this surrender is not made voluntarily and at once, it is effected by suffering. This is the meaning of disease and pain. It is a summons to the lower soul under a flag of truce to surrender.

Consequently, disease and suffering are not an evil, only as we think them such, but a good. What we call evil, as Fichte has said, is the best thing, and the only good thing for some, there is in life. In our inverted condition we call good evil, and evil, good.

Emancipation of the inward and real man from a state of degrading bondage to the body and the senses is the universal remedy for disease. It is not the province of the body to say what I shall be or do; it is for *me* to say. It is said in that remarkable book, *The Perfect Way:* "It is according to the divine order of nature that the soul should control the body. For, as a manifested entity, man is a dual being, consisting of soul and body; and of these in point of duration and function, and therefore in all respects of value, the precedence belongs to the (higher) soul. For the soul is the real, permanent individual, the self, the everlasting, the substantial Idea, of which the body is but the temporary residence and phenomenal expression. The soul, nevertheless, has, properly speaking, no will of her own, since she is feminine and negative. And she is, therefore, by her nature, bound to obey the will of some other than herself. This other can be only the spirit or the body; the Within and the Above, which is Divine, and is God; or the Without and the Below, which, *taken by itself*, and reduced to its last expression, is the *devil*. It is, therefore, to the spirit and soul as one, that obedience is due. Hence, in making the body the seat of the will, the man revolts, not merely against the soul, but against God; and the soul by participation does the same. Of such revolt the consequence is disease and misery of both soul and body." (*The Perfect Way; or, The Finding of Christ*, p. 216.)

"But for this end is the Son of God — the spirit in man, the inward Christ — manifested, that he might destroy the works of the devil," or terminate the dominion of matter and sense, which are one and the same, as all the properties of matter are only sensations in us. (1 John 3 : 8.) Matter is not in itself evil. It is only matter and sense as regnant, that is called the devil, the deceiver. It is the function of the spirit to break the reign of the senses and end their unnatural revolt. To rescue man from this unnatural domination of the lower nature over the higher is the aim of the mental science of disease and the phrenopathic method of cure. In order to effect this, it endeavors to educate men to a higher conception of the dignity and divinity of human nature. The ideas of things are positive, spiritual entities, and belong to the spiritual heavens. Between all the phenomena and appearances of nature and their ideas, there is the relation of effects to their causes. The living ideas of things, which are apprehended only by faith, necessarily precede and control all the phenomena of nature, including the various changes in the body of man. The ideas which we entertain of ourselves, take form first in the psychical body, and through this are ultimated and reflected in the physical body. The condition of the physical organism is only the echo, the reverberation, of our ruling ideas and fixed beliefs. If we would modify the outmost in man, the change must commence in the inmost. Hence the importance of being able to form the correct *idea* of ourselves and to think of ourselves rightly, as thought is the starting point of our existence. If we form an imperfect and distorted idea of ourselves, it will be reflected in the body as certainly, if not as quickly, as when a man distorts his countenance it will appear in the image of himself in the mirror before which he stands. We are commanded to think of ourselves soberly (that is, neither above nor below the true standard), as God hath dealt to each man a measure of faith. (Rom. 12 : 3.) Let us try, then, and take the true measurement of man as a spiritual and immortal being, that the outward body may be fitted to it as a garment of beauty. Some one on being asked how he supposed Jesus looked, replied, "As he thought and felt." That was a comprehensive answer. It has its application to all men, and expresses a profound law of human nature.

What is the divine idea of man? It is said and believed, that God made man in his own image and likeness, and he must have thought of him after the pattern of himself. He has a higher idea of man than he is inclined to form of himself. Man viewed as a material being and weighed in the scales of materialistic science, and even in the popular theological balance, does not count for much, and is hardly worth saving. In opposition to this imperfect view let us weigh man in the balance of the sanctuary, the divine standard, and gain, if possible, the true idea of him. For this true idea will be as a sun. Its living influence will extend from the inmost in us to the outmost by an orderly progression and evolution. "The lamp or lantern of the body is the eye (by which is meant the intellect of the spirit). If the eye be single (that is, sincere, pure), the whole body is lucid. If the eye be evil (or there is a wrong and false idea), the whole body is darkened (or affected by the falsity and the evil). If, then, the luminous principle be darkness, how great is that darkness?" (Matt. 6:22, 23.)

CHAPTER IV.

THE UNCHANGING I AM IN US, OR THE DIVINE AND TRUE IDEA OF MAN.

The great question, "What must I do to be saved?" or healed, in the full sense of the word, is best answered by saying, "Believe in the Lord Jesus Christ, and thou art saved." (Acts xvi: 30, 31.) But the Lord, and the Jesus, and the Christ, are all in man as the centre of his being. They constitute the first *triad*, or first three of the ten Sephiroth, or divine emanations, and are the realm of pure spirit, of which my spirit is a personal limitation. To believe on the Lord Jesus Christ as in me, is equivalent to the intuitive recognition of the truth, that I was never lost except to the consciousness of my lower soul. And thus the Christ within is exalted to be a Prince and a Savior to give repentance unto Israel (or a change of mind or thought, as the word in the original means) for the remission of sin, or the putting away of the errors of understanding. (Acts v: 31.)

There is a region of my conscious being that is not subject to change, and to those ever-varying appearances which characterize the existence of what we call matter, and consequently is not subject to disease or dissolution. I call up in my memory an event of my early childhood. Though my body has wholly changed once a year ever since, and I have passed through a great many vicissitudes of fortune and condition externally, sickness and health, sorrow and joy, yet that which I call *Ego*, the I, the self, is the same I now that it was then. The inner I, the ever-identical Self, has persisted unchanged through all. My thoughts, my sensations, my feelings, desires, volitions, and my environment or surroundings, may have varied at every passing moment of my existence, but *I* have remained the same. This unchanging, undying, and identical self is my spirit, that which Jesus calls in himself the *I am*, and it is that alone which can say of itself, I Am. He who spake as never man spake, says, "I go to prepare a place for you; and if I go and prepare a place for you, I will come again and receive you unto myself, that where *I Am*, there ye may be also — not where I *was* before my incarnation, nor where I shall be after my ascension, but where *I Am*." (John xiv: 1-3.) Again he says: "I will, therefore, that those whom thou hast given me, be with me where *I Am*, not where I *was*, or *shall be*, but in that spiritual state which ever predicates of itself, I Am." (John xvii: 24.) From this region of his being, which knows no past or future, he affirms, "Before Abraham was, *I Am*." (John viii: 57-59.) Now it is evident that Jesus said this of himself as man, for he knew what was in man. (John ii: 25.) This inner unchanging *Ego* is to us a fact of consciousness the most certain of all truths; for no man ever doubted, or can doubt, that his personal or individual identity has remained the same from infancy to age. But that in which our personal identity consists and perpetually persists through all external changes and revolutions, and even successive incarnations, or renewals of the body, is not, and never was, diseased or lost. My sicknesses do not belong to one *Ego*, and my present state of health and blessedness to another. I am the same I, now and forever, and *I Am* not sick or unhappy. Of Jesus the Christ it is affirmed, that he is the same yesterday, to-day, and forever. (Heb. xiii: 8.) It is the Christ within us, whose divine name is Ehejah, or I Am, that is the One and the Same. The Unknown God comes to personal manifestation in the spirit of man. God taught this great lesson which belongs to the greater mysteries, to Moses. In the sacred books of the Persians, the Supreme, the Most High, gives to the seer who asks his name, the answer, *Ahmi*, I Am; and in another place, *Ahmi yat Ahmi*, *I Am that I Am*. This is an old truth. Everything which can predicate of itself, *I am*, is divine, and the highest expression of Divinity, and can never say of itself, *I am* sick or unhappy, for the Ehejah of the Kabala, the Ahmi of the Persians — which is our own inner and divine *self* — may always affirm of itself perfect health and blessedness in the present tense.

If to cure disease is to restore the spiritual life of man, then everything which tends to accomplish that grand result must be considered as the best remedy. I know of nothing, and can conceive of nothing better adapted to this, than the formation in ourselves of the divine and true idea, both of ourselves and of the patient. One of the most marked effects of this method of cure is the development of the spiritual life of the patient, which has long been dormant. Under it we often witness a marked change in his freedom from the dominion of the senses, and the dawning in him of a more spiritual mode of thought and feeling. When a man gains a glimpse of the divine idea of his humanity, and intuitively perceives that the *self* is immortal and undying, and is not and cannot be diseased, he feels an impulse in himself towards the externalization of that idea, or, as Paul would say, "to put on Christ." The Christ within, when discovered to the consciousness of the soul, seeks to clothe itself with a body that perfectly fits it. So when a person thinks that he is a king, he feels an irresistible impulse to act like a king. We may call him insane, but it is only a recognition of what he really is. So as soon as we get the true idea of our real Self, the unchanging and undying *I Am*, and that the real man is not sick, we cannot avoid the consciousness of an impulse to act out the idea and play the part of health.

Whatever mode of thinking will cure me, will, when I think it of another, tend to cure that other. My first aim should be to become perfectly well and happy myself, not from a low, selfish consideration, but from a higher motive. For one of the essential conditions of our being able to cure others by the phrenopathic or spiritual method, is that we be ourselves in health and blessedness; because our *influence*, that is, the inflowing of our minds upon and into another, must of necessity partake of the quality of our mental states, and our inner life. Jesus represented in himself the principle of health, mental and physical. Hence his presence and his touch communicated a sanative contagion. In proportion as we are like him, we can do the same. For a sick man to practise healing, is like a man on crutches showing the world how to walk and run.

When we form in our minds the true idea of a patient, such as he really is in *spirit*, if he is in any degree receptive, we inaugurate a change within him, which will sooner or later work itself outward into a bodily expression. We plant in his unconscious mind the spiritual germ, the living seed of a better condition. This will develop into consciousness in him.

It is a doctrine older than Plato, and an intuitive certainty, that nothing can have an objective existence, or be perceived in the sense-world, before the abstract ideal of that entity is called forth in the mind. Before the mechanic constructs his machine, as a watch or a steam engine, every part of it pre-exists in his mind, and the whole is but the externalization of his ideal. Every object in nature may be reduced to a sensation (which is a feeling) and an idea (which is of the intellect). Without either of these, it has to us no existence. But the idea has an existence prior to the sensation, and without the former the latter could not exist in our consciousness. Hence sensation always arises from within, however contrary this may be to the appearance and the general opinion of men. Professor Müller lays down the general proposition, "*That external agencies can give rise to no kind of sensation which cannot be induced by internal causes exciting changes in the condition of the nerves.*" The sensation of *smell* is sometimes experienced, usually by persons of an excitable, nervous temperament, without the presence of any odorous substance in the air. He affirms that a person blind from infancy, in consequence of the opacity of the transparent media of the eye, may have a perfect internal conception of light and colors. Every one is aware how common it is to see bright colors, and even various objects, while the eye is closed. So of hearing, we know from frequent experience that various sounds are heard, even music, which arise from within, or in the soul itself. (Müller's *Elements of Physiology*, pp. 1059, 1060.)

Vision is possible without the external organ of sight. Even the Scotch metaphysician, Reid, in speaking of the senses, and that we perceive external things through them, for which we can give no reason except that it is the will of God, declares that no man can show it to be impossible to the Supreme Being to have given us the power of perceiving what he calls external objects without such organs. This is what God has done. He has given to every one of us the power to see things in *idea*, or with the mind independent of all organic conditions. This has been taken from the class of hypothetical or supposed things, and demonstrated to be true. On this subject Sir William Hamilton remarks: "However astonishing, it is now proved beyond all rational doubt, that in certain abnormal(?) states of the nervous organism, perceptions are possible through other than the ordinary channels of the senses."

Before anything can exist in the world of sense, it must

have pre-existence as an idea. We may consider this an established principle. As the mechanic forms the watch first as an ideal creation before it becomes an objective reality or actuality, so before we can become well we must form in the mind a distinct idea of the change to be effected in us. We must have the perfect idea of health, and this will act as a cause, for ideas sustain to all the objects of sense a causal relation. In giving treatment to another we must form in our minds a distinct conception, or idea, of the change to be effected in him, and commit this to the Universal Life Principle, the Demiurgic Intellect, the Living Intelligence that forms the world, and all that is in it, and even the human body, after the pattern of pre-existing ideas. Our idea, transferred to the soul of the patient, will become ultimated in a physiological impulse in the direction of the change we desire to inaugurate.

This method of cure conforms to the divine procedure in the formation of the human body, as described in one of the profoundest of the sacred hymns of the Hebrews. "Thou hast formed my reins: thou hast knit me together in my mother's womb. I will give thanks unto thee; for I am fearfully and wonderfully made: wonderful are thy works; and that my soul knoweth right well. My frame was not hidden from thee, when I was made in secret, and curiously wrought in the lowest parts of the earth (or the sub-astral region). Thine eyes (as the symbol of the creative intelligence, the divine imagination, or the idea-forming power) did see mine unperfect substance (the formless cosmic matter), and in thy book (the universal life-principle, the astral light, which contains the record of all that is thought) were all my members written, which day by day were fashioned, when as yet there was none of them." (Ps. cxxxix: 13–16.) This teaches that the body and all its organs were formed in idea before it was ultimated in the sense-world.

When we conform to this method, we act in concert with God.

Man has a body composed of the four elements. This is not man, nor any necessary part of his existence, but belongs wholly to the material world, of which it is a limited expression. In the South Kensington Museum, in England, there is one exhibition which equally interests all classes of visitors. It is a human body resolved into its original elements, or the materials of which the body of man is made. There they all are tied up in packages, or corked up in bottles. Here are so many gallons of water, for three-fourths of the animal body is nothing but that element. But this water is the same that falls in rain and snow. It comes from the external world, and is perpetually returning to it. We have so much chloride of sodium, or common salt. But this is not man, any more than the salt on our tables is man. We have so much carbonate of lime, or marble. This is not man or anything human, any more than the marble slab we place at the head of the grave. So of the iron, the mineral phosphates, and all the solid and gaseous elements. They come from the external world and return to it. An interesting fact regarding them is, that the spectroscope shows the identity of these elements of the human body with the elements which compose the substance of the sun and stars. This fact warrants the assertion of the ancients that man is a microcosm, or little world. The macrocosm, or great world, is only a larger human body, and we a monad or germ cell in it. The body is not man any more than a tree is a man, for a tree in bearing is composed of the same elements.

In this transitory, ever-changing body, the higher intelligence, the distinctively human soul, the *manas*, the real and immortal man, is imprisoned and in chains. It should be our aim to free the living soul from its unnatural subjection to material limitations, and teach it to live even while on earth independent of the body. Forgetting the composite, ever-changing, and consequently mortal body, and renouncing the idea of it as being the man, we represent to ourselves in thought another body, pure, simple, and immortal, created, as it were, within the gross material organism, with a perfect form, and all the members and organs in perfection, with disease and all deformity left out of the conception. This is not a creation of the fancy, but the recognition of a reality. It is the real man, and sustains to the other and lower body, which is no real body, the relation of a sword to the scabbard, and of a precious gem to its casket. But a sword can be withdrawn from the scabbard, and a gem removed from the casket. Until this is done, the one does not accomplish its use, nor the other display its beauty. When the real man is discovered, and we intuitively perceive that it is not what we call the body, any more than a scabbard is a sword, we begin to exercise supernatural faculties, like the newly fledged bird trying its wings. We can go where we please, see without the eye, and hear with the inner ear the sounds of the unseen world, as distinctly as you hear my voice in the phenomenal world. We have begun to live eternal life. We rise out of that region of illusion where disease is possible, into that higher realm where it is impossible. We have passed over that "middle ground," that dangerous region of elemental life, which was represented by the cherubim, which obstruct the approach to the "tree of life." We have passed the guard, and put forth the hand, and eat of the fruit, and live forever.

To emancipate the inward and real man from his imprisonment in matter and an illusory body, is to cure disease. Disease is the translation into a corporeal expression of a wrong or false idea of man. Its cure must commence with the obliteration of that false conception, and the formation of the true idea of ourselves and of the patient. This is the dawning of a new day. After forming the true idea of man, we may give a tacit verbal expression to it by using the following formula, or any form of words that will ultimate the conception.

"In our inmost and true existence and real self, we are not and cannot be diseased, for we are included in the being of the Father of Spirits. Our real life and true being are hid with Christ in God, and our spirit as a manifestation and personal limitation of the Universal Spirit is already immortal in its nature and essence, and disease and pain and sorrow are impossible to it. And this disease (naming the malady, if we desire to do so) is outside of our unchanging and undying personality, and we view it as to us non-existent. We pray the Infinite Father, in the *name* of Jesus Christ, to make us whole. In the silence and stillness of our own soul and will, we pray that Jesus, who represents the only saving, healing principle in the universe, will speak the vivifying inner Word, the Word of life, to the soul of this person; and cause the light of that supreme and eternal truth, which alone can make us free, to illume the darkness of his mind, and liberate the inner man from the fetters of sense and the dominion of sin."

It is important to bear in mind that as thought is the creative principle, and as everything which exists in nature as an objective reality must pre-exist as an idea, so whatever is conceivable in thought is possible. Says Sir William Hamilton: "All necessity is to us, in fact, subjective; for a thing is conceived impossible only as we are unable to construe it in thought. Whatever does not violate the laws of thought is, therefore, not to us impossible, however firmly we may be convinced that it will not occur. For example, we hold it absolutely impossible that a thing can begin to be without a cause. Why? Simply because the mind cannot realize to itself the conception of absolute commencement.

That a stone should ascend into the air, we firmly believe will never happen, but we find no difficulty in conceiving it possible." (*Lectures on Metaphysics*, p. 403.)

This law, that whatever is conceivable is possible, is expressed by Jesus in this way, "If thou canst believe, all things are possible to him that believeth." (Mark ix: 23.) That I should recover from a disease which medical science, so called, pronounces incurable, and become perfectly well, is a possible conception. It contravenes no law of thought. It may, therefore, rationally be an object of faith, and consequently become an actuality. For faith may make actual whatever is possible in thought. When we attain to the true life of faith, things which are impossible to the natural or psychical man become easy of accomplishment.

CHAPTER V.

IS DISEASE A REALITY OR AN ILLUSION?

REALITY has a different meaning from actuality. By actuality is meant the ultimation of an ideal or subjective conception in matter. In that sense a thing may be real and not an actuality.

It is said by Paul, that God hath called us from the beginning, or from the first principle of things, the Logos, or region of an ideal creation, unto salvation in sanctification of the spirit and belief of the truth. (2 Thes. ii : 13.) Sanctification of the spirit is the recognition of the truth that all spirit is a divine substance, and consequently our own spirit, which is the real self, is pure and free from sin and disease. Thus the spirit of life, which is a Hebraism for the living spirit, in Christ Jesus hath made me free from the law of sin and death; that is, the orderly operation of the spirit counteracts the effects of the fixed order of the operation of the errors of the understanding and the delusions of sense. (Rom. viii : 2.)

We attain unto salvation from sin and its consequences in disease and death by the belief of the truth. Now truth expresses that which *is*, in opposition to that which is not, and which only seems to be. An intuitive perception of supersensuous verities, or of truths which lie above and beyond the grasp of the senses, is the ancient and royal road to health and salvation. Jesus, who was himself the way, and the truth, and the life, affirms that we are made free by the knowledge of the truth. (John viii : 32.) But this is not effected by every truth. The mere common verities, or fragmentary truths, as that two plus three are five, and that the angles of a triangle are equal to two right angles, do not save us, though they are sacred and useful. There is a supreme and eternal truth, which includes all other truths in it, and the intuition of this has a saving and redeeming power in it. The highest truth in the universe is that God is all, and all that truly exists is a manifestation of God. (Eph. iv : 6.) The manifested God is the τὸ ἀγαθον of Plato, the Christ of Paul, the supreme and eternal Goodness ; and all things that have true being are an expression of this. All else is illusion, or a false appearance. Nothing can go forth from God that is not always in God. All that *is* is God, and hence is good. That which is not good is not God, and hence has no existence. All that which *is* is included in God. Disease, when viewed as an evil, has no existence except as an illusion or deceptive sensuous appearance. As such it is a nihility, or nothingness.

So far as disease is a condition of the body, like all matter, it is only an appearance, a sensuous seeming, an empty show. The general conclusion of modern philosophy is well stated by Lotze, and is only the reinstatement of the old Hermetic science. He says : " Everything we supposed ourselves to know of matter as an obvious and independent existence, has long since been dissolved in the conviction that matter itself, together with the space, by filling which it seemed most convincingly to prove its peculiar nature, is nothing but an appearance for our perception." (*Metaphysic*, by Herman Lotze, p. 438.)

What we call matter, including the gross material body, has existence only as a false seeming. The supreme reality in the universe is spirit.

Another of those great saving truths, the intuitive perception of which has for the soul a redeeming efficacy, is the inclusion of my true being and immortal self in the Christ, or the universal Spirit. Every universal is made up of particulars, and the particulars are contained in the universal. Every perfect whole is made up of parts, each of which is in the likeness of the whole, and is an image of it. Thus, the body of man is a collection and aggregation of primary cells, each of which is in the form of the entire body. It is the corporeal unit. So there is a universal Spirit, a collective Divine Man, who is the manifested God, and the Christ, and each individual spirit sustains to it the same relation that the cell does to the the human body. The Christ within, which is the particular spirit, as a personal limitation and finite expression of the universal Christ, is an image of the whole, from which it is never sundered. This is the only reality in human nature — all else is illusion. It is the great mystery of the Gospel, and of godliness — God manifested in the flesh, and in my flesh. Of the real Self, the Christ within, we may always predicate perfect health and blessedness. The recognition of this sublime and eternal truth, and a steadfast adherence to it and practical belief of it, is an act of saving faith. It is a divine truth on whose head God has placed a crown, and all sensuous delusions will surrender to it and pay it homage. When Christ, who is our inmost and real life, appears to us and in us, then we also appear with him in glory, and share with him the throne of his glory.

The man that I am in Christ is a different man from the psychical and external homo, the *biped* and *bimanas* animal, the subject of sin and disease. In the world, that is, in the lower and external range of our existence, we have tribulation; but the man that I am in Christ has peace. (John xvi: 33.) No man or religious sect can obtain a monopoly of the great truth, that our inner self is included in the being of the manifested God, the universal Christ, any more than a company could be formed with a charter of incorporation investing them with the exclusive ownership of the sun. I own the sun, and the whole sun, and so does every human being. Every man's spirit is, to speak according to analogy, a cell in the God-Man and the Man-God, and each individual spiritual entity shares the glory of the whole. The universal Spirit, viewed as a collective Divine Human Principle, is called "the Father of spirits," as the atmosphere is the parent source of every breeze and every breath. Whatever Jesus thought and said of his relation to the Father, he has taught every human spirit as an immortal Son of God, to think and affirm of itself. I and my Father are one, for the whole collective life of spirit circulates through each individual spirit. And as nothing impure, or false, or evil, can enter the realm of spirit, or the bosom of the Father, as it is called, so my immortal Ego, whose life is bound up in the same bundle of life with the Father, is free from sin and disease. The Father is in me, and I am in the Father. I came forth from the Father without going out of him, just as a thought or an idea is never external to the mind that thinks. I return to the Father without journeying through space, when I become intuitively conscious that in him I live, and am moved, and have my being.

The Christ within is the God of the microcosmic man, as the Universal Christ is the God of the macrocosm, and thou shalt love the Lord, the God *of thee*, with all thy heart. (Matt. xxii : 37.) This divine spirit in most men only *overshadows* all the lower degrees of our being, like the sun shining above the clouds that conceal him from the earth. If the obstructing vapor becomes etherealized and transparent, then he shines directly upon and into the earth. When the spirit penetrates and pervades with his life all below it in man, even the corporeal organism, then the Christ comes in the flesh, and the man is an incarnation of God. This is the divine ideal becoming the actual, as in Jesus. This is full salvation and perfect health.

Another great spiritual truth, having in it a practical redeeming efficacy, is that of the illusion of the senses. The profoundest and most transcendental teachings of the Oriental religious philosophies, including Buddhism, Brahmanism, Kabalistic Judaism, and esoteric Christianity, are based on the eternal truth, that all our sense-perceptions are an illusion, or deceptive appearance, and our senses never tell us the real truth, but only that which is an inversion of the truth. The directly opposite of the perceptions of the psychical man are true. This is a principle as fixed as that the opposite of darkness is light, and is one of far-reaching practical value. To think rightly, or, in the words of Jesus, to judge righteous judgment, we are to judge and decide directly contrary to the illusory decisions of the sensuous degree of the mind, for it is only in that way that we can come to the cognition of the real truth. This is an established principle in philosophy, and constitutes a pathway of solid rock over which we may walk by faith, from disease to health and blessedness. It is the thread of Ariadne, which, when we trace it back, conducts us out of the labyrinth of error in which we are imprisoned. It is an uphill and shining way, the path of the just, up which we may calmly walk till we reach that mountain summit of health and holiness, from which we have descended into our present lapsed condition.

According to this principle, which is the method of philosophizing called the reconciliation of contradictions, pain is a pleasure misunderstood. The psychical man or mind falsely views it as an evil, and by thinking so, makes it an evil. But pain is always a good, and all good is in its nature and essence pleasant and delightful. This is what all men mean by the word good. A boil is not an evil, much less a disease, but a good thing. When I no longer view it as an evil, but a good, then the pain ceases, for all good is a pleasure. A thing is to us what we *think* and *believe* it to be.

In accordance with the principle we are discussing, loss is gain, disease is health, sorrow is joy, and death is life. Disease is an effort of the divine life-principle in us in the direction of true health. Nausea is only an effort of nature, the divine *Archœus* of Van Helmont, to rid the stomach of something antagonistic to the life-principle in us. Hence the action of the stomach is inverted. If this does not succeed, nature intensifies and accelerates the natural peristaltic action of the stomach and intestinal canal, and a diarrhœa is the result, which is not a disease or an evil, only as we make it so by our way of thinking. It is a device of nature to rid the system of that which is injurious. The body is often renewed and rejuvenated by a fever; and a fever is not a disease, but a remedy. It is not an evil, but a good, and all good is pleasant. As death, according to Swedenborg, is not the extinction of life, but a higher exhibition of it which is called *anastasis*, or resurrection, so disease, which precedes death and leads to it, signifies that which is progressive to regeneration or newness of life. (*Arcana Celestia*, 6221.) This, he affirms, is the signification of disease among the angels, and consequently it bears this meaning to the higher intelligence of man; for Swedenborg's angels, like Milton's, are only a superior kind of men. Disease is always a remedy. And if as a phenomenon or appearance, it is so interpreted by the light of the spirit, and not by the darkness and blindness of sense, it will essentially change its nature and effects.

What we call sorrow is not so only in name. It is always the memory of a joy that has passed out of present consciousness, but not out of existence. No state of joy, or peace, or health, that we have ever experienced, is lost, or ever can be lost, to our being. It may have passed out of the present consciousness of the soul, but according to the Buddhist doctrine of *karma*, and the Swedenborgian doctrine of *remains* (*reliquiæ*, or relics), it is stored up in us as an everlasting inheritance. Our early states of youthful bliss and health, and all the innocent joys of childhood, have not been obliterated from the imperishable tablet of the higher soul, but have only gone to seed, and are treasured up in our interiors as living germs, that only need the dews of heaven to cause them to spring up again in a larger harvest. They can be made to emerge into consciousness, and be remitted from the interior into the exterior or psychical man. In this sense, by an immutable law of our being, what we have sown we shall sometime reap, and with an increase. The cure of disease in ourselves or others is a *recovery*, or a restoration to the consciousness of the lower soul of that which has passed inward, and has been reserved in the interiors of man by the Lord of life, but has not dropped out of existence. To view it in that light is the best way to call it back again. Health is within; and if we look for it in any other place, we miss it. It will be like searching the forests to find a lost child, when he is all the time asleep in his chamber. If we had only known where he was to be found, all our search abroad would have been avoided. To cure disease is to restore to the soul that state of health which we mourn as lost, but which is still in the higher apartment of our being. "He restoreth my soul, and guideth me in the paths of righteousness (or spiritual truth) for his name's sake." (Ps. xxiii : 3.)

Another fundamental truth of the Hermetic philosophy, and which brings freedom to the soul of man, is, that matter (in its reality), like spirit, is exempt from disease and corruption. Spirit and matter are the two extreme links in the chain of existence. They are co-eternal and co-extensive, and equally divine. Like the two forces of the magnet, the positive and the negative, each implies the other, and neither can exist without the other. But we are not speaking of what men in general call matter, but of a divine *substance*. Between the two extreme links of existence, spirit and matter, the first and the last, the Alpha and the Omega, the Father and the Mother, all other existences are situated. The phenomenon which we call matter is but an illusion. It is not substance, but a deceptive appearance. The real body of man is never diseased, for in its essence it is a divine, an indestructible, and immortal substance. *It is the Bride of the Spirit.* If the Spirit of man is not diseased (and this is admitted), and if the body as to its invisible inward essence is pure and free from disease and corruption, then we ask, What is disease but an illusion of the senses, a false appearance, that ought to count for nothing? It is among the certainties that disease is not the reality it passes current for in an unbelieving world. Matter as the pure *cosmic substance*, the divine Mother principle, is as immortal as spirit, of which it is the correlative opposite and necessary counterpart in the creative balance.

What is called dirt and filth is only so to a superficial gaze and shallow way of thinking. What we call filth, in its inner essence, its divine chemistry, is as pure as the diamond, or the precious stones which constitute the foundation of the walls of the New Jerusalem. As filth is not filth except to the stupid gaze of ignorance, and as a false opinion of things is the only dirt in the universe, so disease has existence only as a misbelief. It has existence neither in the spirit of man, nor in the real substance of the body. And as all existence is included in the grasp of these extremes, it must be viewed as non-existent.

In the phrenopathic method of cure the question will often recur, What is man? And the answer will always be in order, that man is a being made in the image of God, and only a little while inferior to the angels, and crowned with glory, and honor, and immortality. (Ps. 8 : 4-6.) Certainly the outward body, though fearfully and wonderfully made, is not man; for when the mortal coil is shuffled off, nothing has been lost. The five external senses are not man, for these belong wholly to the body. The mind, on the plane of sense, the mere animal soul taken by itself, does not answer to the idea of man. The distinctively human principle is spiritual, immortal, and incorruptible. As disease and sin are in the lower soul, and as this is not man, it follows that these are not predicable of the true self. Man, that is, that which is the distinctively human principle and undying personality, that which is more than an animal, is neither sick nor sinful. When through love and faith, which penetrate to that within the veil, we recognize the good that is in man, and are blind to the evil that is external to the real humanity, it serves to develop that good. It craves recognition, and is in an effort to make itself known. And when recognized in some mind, it strengthens its tendency to an ultimate manifestation. This seems to have been what Jesus did. He recognized good in publicans and sinners, and condemned none, and thus lifted from them the millstone that was sinking them into the depths. In the physical wrecks around him he beheld only the inner man, and addressed himself to that. When we recognize that in man which is immortal, and consequently never sick, it serves to develop that also. It opens the prison to them that are bound, and sets the captive free.

> "Let's find the sunny side of men,
>   Or be believers in it:
> A light there is in every soul
>   That takes the pains to win it.
> Oh! there's a slumbering good in all,
>   And we perchance may wake it;
> Our hands contain the magic wand:
>   This life is what we make it."

"And when the Christ that is in us is raised from the dead, he dieth no more; death no more hath dominion over him. For in that he died, he died unto sin once for all; but in that life that he liveth, he liveth unto God. Even so reckon ye yourselves to be dead unto sin, but alive unto God in Christ Jesus." (Rom. 6 : 9–11.)

Reality expresses what *is;* illusion is what only *appears* to be. The human body is not man, and its diseases are no part of our true humanity. Owing to the dominating influence of the senses, we accept appearances for realities, and take the shadow of man for the man himself. This is the fundamental error of the world. But when a man, suffering from disease, sees through the glimmering light of the supreme knowledge that the external body is not the self, but is the most unreal thing in human nature, and that his disease is outside his immortal self, it is like returning light to the blind, or like the first break of day after the long Arctic night. In a fragment of the books of Hermes, it is said, "Mundane things (which include the body and its maladies) are not themselves real, but only the simulacra of reality, and not all are even such; some are but illusion and error, fantastic appearances, mere phantoms. When such an appearance receives an influx from above, then, indeed, it becomes a similitude of the real; but without this superior influence, it remains an illusion. In the same way a portrait is a painted image of a body, but is not the body it represents. It appears to have eyes, but sees nothing; ears, but hears nothing; and so on of the rest of it. It is an image which deceives the sight; it appears a reality, and is but a shadow. Those who behold not the false behold the true. If, then, we understand and see every thing as it truly is, we see the real; but if we see that which is not, we can neither understand nor know anything of the real."

CHAPTER VI.

THE FALL AND THE REDEMPTION, OR THE FUNDAMENTAL EVIL
IN HUMAN NATURE, AND THE REMEDY.

The fall of man was not the result of any single act of disobedience to the divine will, as the eating of some forbidden fruit, but was rather the gradual descent of man in the scale of life and thought, from a spiritual altitude or plane of existence, into a condition of bondage to the external senses, and to the limitations of time and space. How great was this subsidence of the life of man few can comprehend, because the height from which human nature has descended to its present sensuous level is beyond the conception of the psychical man. The fall is a total inversion of the divine order of life. That which is divine and immortal in man, the spirit, which is the seat of all the deific powers of man, is brought into subjection to the body, and is fettered in its action by the limitations of matter. The original condition of man is symbolically represented by his being placed in the garden of Eden, which the Lord planted in the *East*, which signifies the realm of pure spirit, which is the true Orient, the arising, the origin of all things; and the garden into which the "Lord God" put man, signifies the clear intuitions of celestial love, a perception of truth derived from the Lord *in* man. By the Eloheim is meant the God who creates and governs the world, the macrocosmic universe. By the Adonai, or Lord, is signified *our* God, or deific centre, the divine spirit in man. To eat of the tree of life is to perceive and recognize the truth that all life and all intelligence are from the Lord, and are the Lord in man.

To eat of the tree of knowledge (external, carnal knowledge) represents symbolically the life of sense, which is accompanied with the feeling that our intelligence and life are self-derived.

To understand more clearly the nature of the fall and the redemption, we remark that there is in us an internal and an external man. The latter is composed of what is usually denominated the body, the gross material organism, and the astral soul, the *nephesh* of the Jewish psychology, the lowest animal nature. These two are but the shadow of man. The external is the mortal man, for at death the corporeal organism and the *anima bruta* are thrown off. These are not of necessity evil, only as they come to dominate over the higher nature. The internal man, in its highest degree, is divine, immortal, and celestial. In the fall of man the due relations between the internal and external man are subverted. The governing will is transferred from the spirit, which is the highest in man, to the body, which is the lowest. From this inversion of the true order of our existence, sin, disease, and all our misery have entered into the world. The redemption of man is the reversion of this order. The sceptre is wrested from the body and the animal soul, and the divine spirit of man is reinstated in its rightful governance of the whole human kingdom. When the inner man, the spirit, regains its rightful control of the body, man has attained "the crown of life," and is exempt from disease, and even death. By redemption, then, we mean a deliverance from the controlling influence of the body and the astral soul, and it is only because man has fallen under the dominion of the body and the animal senses, that he needs redemption.

But how is this consummation, so devoutly to be wished, to be attained? Can any light be thrown upon the path that unerringly conducts to it? Is there no way out of our misery? Is there no remedy for the ills to which our life on earth is constantly liable? Is the key that opens the prison lost?

It is said of Gautama, who did for the East what Jesus, six hundred years later, did more fully for the West, that he sought long and earnestly, and with extreme ascetic mortifications, which proved of no avail, for the *cause* of all human misery. At last the light from the supreme heavens broke in upon him, and his mind became entirely opened, "like the full-blown lotus-flower," and he saw by an intuitive flash of the supreme knowledge, that the secret of all the miseries of mankind was *ignorance;* and the sovereign remedy for it was to dispel ignorance and to become wise. If this is not the key that unlocks our dungeon, it shows where the lock is to be found.

The teaching of the Buddha is here identical with the principles of esoteric Christianity. In the religious philosophy of Jesus the cause of disease and all misery is sin, an aberration or deflection from the truth, as the original word is defined in the Greek lexicons. The word is used in the New Testament in the sense given to it by Plato, as an error of the understanding, which may lead to wickedness in the life. Paul teaches the same doctrine as both Jesus and Plato and Gautama had taught in regard to the root of human misery. He enjoins upon the Christians of Ephesus, that they no longer walk, that is, live, as the Nations walk, in the vanity (or illusion) of their mind, being darkened in their understanding, and alienated from the life of God because of the ignorance that is in them. (Eph. iv: 17, 18.) The remedy for this is *faith*, a spiritual enlightenment which gives the perception of real truth. The ignorance, which is the underlying cause of all our misery, is not merely a want of knowledge, nor is it a lack of what is called science, for that is only a sensuous knowledge, the superficial observation of facts, but it is a total inversion of the real truth. Through this sin, or inversion of the truth, we are led to consider that as real which is only a false seeming; and that which is the real and the enduring we deem an illusion and a phantom; and we are influenced to desire and laboriously seek as our highest good, and object of supreme quest, that which is of no worth, and even hurtful. In this dense ignorance the body is viewed as the man. The shadow is taken for substance. The existence of the higher soul is doubted or denied, and the being of the spirit is wholly unknown. Our sense-perceptions, which are always illusory and a deceptive appearance, are accepted without question, and their fallacious testimony is received as the highest and most certain form of knowledge. Matter, or what we call matter, which is not *substance*, but is the most unreal thing in the universe, is exalted into the place of God in our thoughts, and made the all in all of existence. This is the essence of idolatry.

In this fallen and inverted condition, which is a hot-bed of disease and all evil, influx from the lower region of the world of spirits, as it is called by Swedenborg, the astral plane of life, the region of undeveloped elemental and elementary souls, has a preponderating influence in the life of man. These are the "demons" of the Platonic philosophy and of the New Testament, which Jesus "cast out" from those he healed. Influx from this disorderly realm intensifies the tendency to any morbid condition of the mind and body, and like a dark cloud between us and the sun, shuts out the inflowing of light and life from the world of pure spirit, the region of the supreme and saving knowledge. The deliverance of man from this condition, and the readjustment of his relations to the spiritual world, is an important preliminary act in our redemption; for man can be saved only in perfect freedom. The dispersion of the elementary or astral influences, and the placing of man in a position where he can receive influx from the realm of spirit, or the Universal Christ, is called a day of judgment or separation, and this has been effected for the world. This region or sphere of astral souls, the highest of whom are symbolized by the four-faced Cherubim, comes between us and the sun of a higher sky, as a dense fog obscures the light of day, and veils the heavens from our view. How can we be saved from their overmastering influence? Oftentimes prayer, the tranquil aspiration of the soul towards the Highest and the Best, and a resolve "to know nothing but the Christ," is our most effectual remedy. The soul is "like an infant crying for the light, and with no language but a cry." Every night is followed by its morning. Jesus cast out the spirits by "the Word" — a condensed expression of the Supreme and Eternal Truth, which formulates itself in the Universal Living Principle.

Our redemption or liberation from corporeal bondage, is not effected by the passion of the cross, nor by anything external, but always comes from *within*. It is a development of our inmost and real Self. The spirit in us, which is the inward Christ, and which is always in accord with the Universal Spirit, who is the Father, being reinstated in his rightful dominion over all below it in man, even the body, is the redeemer. We do not mean by this that man is or ever can be redeemed without God. The divine spirit in man is never separated from the manifested God, who is called the Christ. It acts in and from the Father. And it is the Christ principle alone that can deliver us from the power of darkness (or the life of sense), and translate us into the kingdom of God's dear Son (or into the reign of the immortal spirit in us). Through the blood of the Christ (the living truths of the spirit) we have redemption, even the remission of our sins (or the putting away of the illusions of the sensuous animal soul). (Eph. i : 7. Col. i : 12–14.) If it is this alone which can dispel the darkness of the psychical man, and give us freedom from our bondage, how may we obtain the perception of this supreme, saving truth? That is the great question which thousands will ask me to solve. Fortunately, the answer is not difficult.

Truth corresponds to light, and is represented by it, because light in the world of nature is truth in the realm of mind. The bondage to the senses, which is the general state of mankind, with its errors and fallacious appearances, each of which is a fetter of the soul, is called darkness, and in this condition man is represented as in chains of darkness. The lower soul of man is the basement story of our existence. If the basement story of our dwelling is dark and dank, we open a window from *within*, and the light, by a law of its nature, comes in and illumes the darkness, — or it appears to come in, — but in reality is developed from within. So if we throw open the windows of the soul, removing the bars and bolts from within, the celestial light of truth will flow in and enlighten the darkness of error into which we are plunged, and which is the spring of all our disease and misery. The world is under the powerful dominion of phantasy or illusion. It is only the living truths of the spirit, the region in us of intuition, and the ineffable light of the supreme knowledge, which is mystically called the blood of the Christ, that can disenchant us. Our inmost Spirit and undying Self represents to us the Universal Christ, who, like the Buddha, is the All-Knowing One, and the principle and source of enlightenment in us. The sole condition of receiving this saving truth and living light of the heavens is the *desire* for it. Truth, grounded in the affections, will grow into an intuitional enlightenment, a permanent state of insight. God is Light, and the centre whence emanates the supreme effulgence of truth. If we adore him as such, we shall behold him. Truth in us is never separated from God.

> "God dwelleth in a light far out of human ken;
> Become thyself that light, and thou shalt see him then."

Every successive advance of man, as a collective race or as an individual, is a progressive approach to the true vision or understanding of God. When that vision is attained, and man is revealed to himself, our development is complete and our salvation full; for to know God, and to know our Self as included in him, is eternal life. We cannot know him as external to our inward Self; for that which has not something in me that answers to it, is unknowable. The Lord, the Adonai of the Old Testament, is *my* God, and my inmost divine self and life, and as such cannot be diseased or sinful.

The celestial heavens, the realm of saving truth, the light of life, are not far off from our inner being. Things may seem outwardly distant, but may nevertheless be inwardly near. Everything exists for us in thought. That of which we do not think has for us no existence. That of which we think, exists in us, and if we desire and love it, we exist in it. It is as near to us as our thought of it, which is never outside of our own minds. Nothing seems further from the psychical man, and from the earth, than heaven. Yet to the spiritual man or mind nothing is nearer to him and to the earth than heaven. The central point of our existence is in the kingdom of the heavens. The domain of the spirit in us is the kingdom of God in man of which Jesus speaks.

The law which governs the influx of saving, healing truth, and its reception by us, is given by Jesus in the Sermon on the Mount, "Blessed are they who hunger and thirst after righteousness: for they shall be filled." (Matt. v: 6.) The Kabalistic righteousness, or justice, symbolized by the perfect square, which means perfection, is a state of spiritual enlightenment, the attainment of the gnosis, or true knowledge, which makes us free. It is a principle which seems to extend through the whole universe, that a demand, a conscious need, creates a supply. Hence it is said, "The prayer (δέησις, desire, from a sense of want) of a righteous (or spiritually enlightened) man availeth much in its working." (James v: 16.) The original term expresses the idea that such a prayer, or desire, is a positive spiritual energy. The desire, the will, the wish to live the life of sense and of earthly pleasure, becomes an attraction of the soul in that direction. The things we desire gravitate towards us and we towards them. An inordinate desire for life in the world, with all its selfish gratifications, draws the disembodied soul into the sphere of the earth even after death. In accordance with this law of our being, and of being in all worlds, a desire for the life of the spirit, as contra-distinguished from the fleshy life of sense, a desire for the celestial and immortal range of existence on earth, becomes in us an inward impulse in that direction. If we have not this, nothing can be done for us: we are impervious to the light of life. Jesus said of the sensuous Jews of his day: "Ye will not (that is, wish not, desire not) to come unto me, that ye might have life." (John v: 40.) If we have this desire and inward attraction, it adjusts the soul and all her powers into a state of receptivity, — a peaceful vacuum which the ever-present heavens make haste to fill. A desire for the supreme, saving truth constitutes an affinitive attraction between the soul and that truth, as real as that which exists between the lodestone and iron.

Men instinctively desire deliverance from the unnatural domination of the body and the animal soul, for all feel this to be a condition of degradation; in other words, a fall from the true position we were made to occupy. The bodily senses, by their phantasms, have so clouded the higher soul of man as to obscure his inner life, and obstruct the free development of our true being. But as long as there is a desire for deliverance there is a ground for hope. Hope is born of desire, and "faith is the substance of things hoped for." In the Epistle to the Romans, Paul declares that we who have the first fruits of the spirit (or the incipiency of the spiritual state of our powers) groan within ourselves, waiting for the adoption (the recognition of our individual spirit as the immortal Son of God in us), the redemption from the body. (Rom. viii : 23.) This does not refer to the incredible dogma of a literal resurrection from the graveyard, but to a state of emancipation from material and corporeal thralldom attainable here and now. It is a deliverance of the inner man from the controlling influence of the body. The first ray of hope comes to us with the clear intuition of the truth that the body has no power of its own. It is in its nature entirely passive and inert, and its normal function is to express and obey the spirit. It is no part of man, any more than a brazen statue is a human being. It has no power, except as by a wrong way of thinking we attribute power to it; and this is a delusion, a false belief. If it is true that the body has no power, then why are we so dependent upon it, and become the veriest slaves to it? It is a sort of idolatry into which we have fallen, like the investing of a senseless block of wood or stone with divine attributes. To attribute to gross matter what only belongs to the divine spirit in us, is like crowning a lifeless image of a man as an emperor and paying homage to it. In that case, the phantastic image, the *eidolon*, has no authority except what we give to it. It can neither utter a command nor enforce it. So the material body has no life of its own, and no power over us, except what we in thought ascribe to it. When we cease to do this, our full redemption draws near.

The normal relation of the body to the inner and real man

was clearly seen by Swedenborg, and is well stated by him in one of the profoundest of his philosophical works. "It is well known that the will and the understanding govern the body at pleasure; for the mouth speaks what the understanding thinks, and the body does what the will determines; hence it is evident that the body is a form corresponding to the understanding and the will; and as form is also predicated of the understanding and the will, it is evident that the form of the body corresponds to the form (by which is also signified state, quality) of the understanding and the will." (*Divine Love and Divine Wisdom*, 136.)

Again he says: "There are gestures and actions of the body which correspond to every affection of the mind, as falling down on the knees corresponds to humiliation, and prostration to the earth to deeper humiliation; the spreading out of the hands towards heaven corresponds to supplication, and so forth; those gestures or actions in the Word signify the affections themselves to which they correspond, because they represent them; hence it may be seen what is meant by representations." (*Arcana Celestia*, 7596.)

The tendency of thought and feeling to express themselves outwardly in gesture or some visible motion or attitude of the body is only an exhibition of the operation of a universal law. Thought and feeling are not only spontaneously expressed or represented in visible gestures, but also in invisible vital and physiological movements and activities of the various internal organs. If we form in our minds the true idea of ourselves as already immortal and free from disease and sin, it is the function of the body to express that idea, not in words, gestures, and attitudes merely, but in a condition corresponding to it, and which is a translation of it into a corporeal representation. Before things can exist in the sense-world, or as actualities, the *ideas* of them as subjective realities and typical forms must subsist. For a thing, be it a tree, a stone, a statue, a house, or a physical malady, is the externalization of an idea without which it cannot exist. In attaining to a state of redemption from the body we must determine in our minds what is the divine idea of man, and the body will conform to that idea and surrender to it. It is self-evident that an infinitely good and wise Creator could not form the plan of our life that should not be in harmony with himself. The divine idea of man is not one that includes in it the typical representation of man as diseased, sinful, and unhappy.

There is a principle in man, or a primordial substance, which lies in absolute subjection to the will of the spirit. It is the astral body, and is that on which the gross material phantom is dependent for its existence. It is that which is denominated by Paul, the *psychical* body, — as being the body of the soul, — and which has been grossly mistranslated the "natural body." "There is a psychical body, and there is a spiritual body." (1 Cor. xv: 44.) The spirit of man does not act directly on the external body, the gross physical organism, but on this intermediate principle, and through that moves and affects the outward shell. Every particle of this psychical body and elemental substance is capable of responding with instantaneous celerity to the dictates of the sovereign will of the spirit. As a lake reposing in stillness among the hills, in a clear night and beneath a cloudless sky, mirrors and reflects the stars and planets and all the objects above it in the heavens, so this passive substance reflects and responds to the ideas in our minds. As the stars with "mimic glory" shine in the water, and are mirrored in its placid surface, so the real knowledges of things, the true ideas of God and man, will become expressed in the body.

The man who can steadfastly *think* the truth in regard to his real being has the key that unlocks the handcuffs of his soul, and his immortal powers are set free. The spirit of man, the real self, is safe from sin and disease. Secure in its stronghold on the heights of Divinity, and immortal in every part, though assailed and besieged by a crowd of sensuous illusions and phantoms more numerous than the army of Senacherib which approached Jerusalem and Zion, it may rest in peace, like the Southern Cross in the heavens. Until that can be plucked down from the firmament and laid in the dust, we as immortal spirits cannot be dislodged from our dwelling place in the life of God. The spirit of man is so intermingled and interblended with the existence of the Father, that by a supreme act of faith it may ever say, "Because he lives, I live; because he is free from disease, so am I." Though the body may be put off and become a wreck, and be dissolved back into its original elements, yet the redeemed soul may view it, not as death, but as the wreck of the shell out of which an angel is born. For it is a law as universal as the presence of God in nature, that out of what the world falsely calls death there is always evolved a higher form and order of life. There is no death. All is boundless, endless, omnipresent, and omniactive life. As death is an illusion or deceptive appearance, so is disease when viewed from the lofty altitude of an assured faith. To the touch of Christian faith, the empty bubble which appears to the mind on the plane of sense a solid reality, bursts and becomes a crystal drop of the water of life. A minister remarked at the funeral of a neighbor of ours a few days ago, that it was difficult for the natural man to feel that he was going to die. That may be true, but it is more difficult for the psychical man or mind to realize the truth that he will never die, and that the diseases of men are only a struggle of the soul into immortality on earth and in the heavens. Disease is the dream that precedes and occasions our waking into life. It is the shock that comes to startle us from the slumber of a life of sense, an alarm-clock that is set to wake us at break of day.

CHAPTER VII.

THE GLORIFICATION OF OUR HUMANITY, OR FULL SALVATION FROM SIN AND DISEASE.

WE are told by Paul that those who seek for glory and honor and incorruption have their search rewarded by the discovery of eternal life, not in an indefinite and distant future, which has no existence, but in the divine moment, the ever-present and eternal now. The word glory, in its popular acceptation, signifies an external brightness, a sort of dazzling splendor. But besides its exoteric or common meaning, it has a deeper esoteric meaning, as Plato in the *Cratylus* has more than hinted. The word for glory in the original language of the New Testament is derived from a verb which means to think. In this interior sense, the word glory signifies the highest state of *inward illumination*. To glorify God is to think well and rightly of him. To glorify our humanity is to attain to the true conception of it, as an incorruptible and immortal divine manifestation. The inward and real self, the I Am, is recognized as identical with the "Lord." This is the final secret which God holds in reserve for those who love him, and to be made known to them in the fulness of time, or when in the progress of our spiritual unfoldment the auspicious moment arrives. The Christ, as I have often said in the preceding pages, is the manifested God, the first emanation from the "Unknown," a manifestation of God as the Universal Man, or a Divine Human Principle, and this God in us is the Lord. The Lord is *our* God, the God of the microcosmic man as well as of the macrocosmic universe. He is Immanuel, which is, being interpreted, God *in* us, and as constituting our inner and true *self*. Hence, as Al Ghazzali, in his *Alchemy of Happiness*, quoting the ancient prophets or spiritual teachers, has said, "He who knows himself, knows his Lord also." And we might affirm that he who truly knows the Lord, comes also to the true knowledge of the self, for the two are one and the same.

This glorification of our humanity is the highest condition of "grace." This word, like the word glory, has an esoteric signification. In its exoteric or external acceptation, it means mercy and favor; but in its Kabalistic sense, it means the secret teaching of the masters. It came to have this meaning in this way: they took the two Hebrew words for "hidden wisdom," which was a designation of the Kabala, and from the initials of the two a third word was formed, and that is the word for grace. Hence, grace signifies the occult spiritual wisdom, which Paul spake only to the "perfect" or fully instructed. This gives the full meaning to many passages of the New Testament. "By grace ye are saved;" that is, we attain to salvation by the knowledge of the supreme truth that lies beyond the ken of the psychical man. It is said in the Gospel of John, that the *law*, or the external system of truth, came by Moses; but *grace* and truth came by Jesus the Christ. (John i: 17.)

Jesus came to do for the world at large, by revealing the sublime wisdom of the ancient mystical sects and brotherhoods, what had been done only to the chosen few in the sacred privacy of the inner recesses of the temples. But Jesus, whose maxim was, "there is nothing hid that should not be revealed" for the benefit of mankind, has done this more fully than was ever done to the initiate in the sacred mysteries. And may this "grace" of our Lord Jesus Christ be with us. (Rom. xvi: 20.) And may we grow in the grace and knowledge of our Lord Jesus Christ, the Savior, or Health-Giver. (2 Peter iii: 18.) For the true knowledge of Jesus is the most important of all knowledge attainable by the mind and heart of man. In his triple name he represents to us the first divine triad of the Ten Sephiroth, or emanative principles. He is the divine exemplar, or model humanity, showing to all ages and races of men the possibilities of the spiritual development of man. For what he attained, our human nature may reach. This he plainly teaches. (John xiv: 3; xvii: 24.) He was the Christ, and we may be raised to the Christ-sphere of life. This is implied in our becoming truly Christian. For the word Christian is but a diminutive of Christ. He is the Jah or Yah, the divine Yes, the Amen, the pure intelligence, the Nous of the Greeks. (2 Cor. i: 20.) This is the second emanative principle, and is called the Lord. Kurios, the Greek name for Adonai or Lord, was viewed by the ancients as the God-Mind, a divine intelligence in the world. Plato, in the *Cratylus*, says that " Kurios signifies the pure and unmixed nature of intellect."

He is the Yava, the Jehovah of the Old Testament, the third emanation from the "Unknown," the perfect union of pure intelligence with pure love; and as such is the Savior, or Health-Giver, to the souls and bodies of men. The Jehovah of the Old Testament is identical with the Hebrew name of Jesus, and in Jesus the word is translated into its true significance, and thus freed from the horrible perversions of its meaning in exoteric Judaism. In Jesus, Jehovah becomes once more to men, not a Deity to be feared, but the Bon Dieu, the Good God, to be loved and trusted with all the heart.

There are many sincere people who are inquiring the way to a true spiritual life, or to an habitual mode of thought and feeling that raises us above the plane of the psychical man, and which shall give them lordship over the senses and the body. But our deliverance is to be sought within ourselves. A right understanding of that remarkable saying of Jesus, "I am the *Way*, the *Truth*, and the *Life*," will place all such persons in the "path." It is not the mere historic Jesus, the son of Joseph and Mary, but the Christ in him, who here speaks. The Christ, as the indwelling Word, is the only principle and source of divine illumination and spiritual intelligence. This is to be sought in the depths of our own inner being, for in us is the Word of life and the Light of the world, and the only light that can be shed upon our path. If it cannot be discovered, or uncovered here, it can be found by us nowhere. Paul speaks of the great mystery, or hidden truth of the Gospel, and which had been concealed from the generations of the past ages, but which was then made known to men as Christ *in* you, the hope of glory, or as the ground of our exaltation to a state of inward illumination, or a truly spiritual condition of our intellectual powers. The mystic brotherhoods of the past and the present are only a dark lantern to the world. Christianity came to break the opaque envelope and let their imprisoned light out. He who has sought and found the Christ within, and has risen above the conception of him as an external, historical person, and has identified his inmost self with him, is in the way to know all that was ever known of spiritual truth by the mind of man, for it is all there still. For in the Christ are hid all the treasures of wisdom and knowledge. (Col. ii : 3.) He is on the threshold of becoming more than man, as Jesus did. He is about to realize the truth of the passage, "I said ye are gods, and all of you are sons of the Most High," or the Divine Inmost. (Ps. lxxxii : 6. John x : 34.) The Christ in his fulness includes in himself the inmost degree of my own being. And it is this in me which ever affirms of itself *I am*, that is, the way and the truth, and the life. Hence says the Christ, "If any man thirst (or desire spiritual truth), let him come unto me (in thought) and drink, and the water that I shall give him shall be in him a fountain of water springing up into (and from) everlasting life." (John iv : 14.) The Christ within is the way, and the truth, and the life, all in one. He who has entered into the way will be gradually conducted to the end, for it will be the path of the *just*, that shineth more and more unto the perfect day. This *end* involves in it an intuitive perception of the absolute unity of God, and that we are somehow included in that unity. For if Christ, as the manifested God, is the essential Truth and the essential Life, then it follows that so far as I am in these, I am in Christ, and Christ liveth in me. My being has become indissolubly involved in his; my isolated selfhood, or proprium, has disappeared and become united to the Supreme Self. When the sun rises, the dew-drop is taken up into a shining sea of light. It is not lost, not annihilated, but glorified.

When the Invisible God, the Supreme Divine Essence, as the Absolute Being, who is beyond the reach and grasp of thought, would pass outward into existence, or become manifested in creation, he goes forth in the *form* of man, which is a Divine Humanity, the Maximus Homo, or greatest man, the Adam Kadmon of the Kabala. In the Hindu theosophy, the Aditi, the boundless, becomes Viradj, the Divine Man. As Swedenborg affirms from an older philosophy, God is seen by the angels in a human *form*, which means human quality and not merely shape. Not that he is seen externally, for nothing in heaven or earth is ever seen externally to the mind by men or angels. The pure in heart see God in themselves *and as the real self.* For in man the Invisible becomes visible, the Unknown becomes known, the Impersonal becomes personal, the Infinite becomes definite by self-limitation, and the Formless and Nameless takes form and name. Thus the highest expression and revelation of God is the inmost *self* of man. And this can always affirm, "I and my Father are one."

Christ as the manifested God, the God-Man, is our inmost and verimost life. (Col. iii: 4.) If we can find this, we can find him, and discover the point where our life blends with God's life — where the Divine becomes human, and the human, Divine. This inward Christ, when manifested in the flesh and dominating all the physiological organs and functions, is the *Lord*, who is the strength of our life and the "health of our countenance." (Ps. xlii: 11.) Christ is also made unto us wisdom or intuitive knowledge, and our wisdom is Christ, as its connection with him is never broken. He is our righteousness, our faith or spiritual truth. To be saved by faith is to be saved by Christ, for faith is the Christ in us. In being saved by faith from sin and disease, there is no miracle, but as the London *Lancet* has said, "it would be a miracle if, the organism being constituted as it is, and the laws of life such as they are, faith-healing, under favorable conditions, did not occur." Christ within is our sanctification and redemption. He is not merely our redeemer, but our redemption itself. He is not merely a Savior or Health-Giver, as if he were a power outside of us who comes to our rescue, but he is our health and our salvation. *His merit is our merit, as being a quality of the inner self which is inseparable from him.* We are not to view him as an historic person about whose life we read in the Gospel narratives, but as a universal divine-human principle, ever present in, and never absent from, the inner recesses of our being.

We are to expunge from our minds the hurtful conception and sense of *separateness*, or the feeling of the isolation of the individual spirit from that universal Spirit of which it is a limitation. The inward man is an epitome of the Christ. For in man the manifested God divides himself without diminishing himself.

In order to come into the closest union with God, we must be able to form in our minds the true *idea* of him. God is a Spirit, and our spirit is in the image and likeness of God, or is the idea of God in us. That idea is my inner self, and it is also God in man. And things which are equal to the same thing are equal to one another. They who worship God must worship him *in spirit* (our own spirit) and *in truth*. (John iv : 24.) To adore him under a false conception of him is to adore a false God, which is all the same as no God, for falsity is equivalent to nonentity. The ancients supposed the resemblance of a thing or being was animated by the life of that which it resembled, and as man is an express image of God, he is pervaded with a divine vitality. An image or statue of a man, as of a Washington or Lincoln, is an external expression of our idea of them ; and if it be a high work of art and a worthy resemblance, it seems as we look at it to be animated by them. On this subject a Hermetic volume, published in 1650, says : " Those men who are skilled in the secrets of the theology of the ancients, assure us, that those who first set up images in their temples, resembling the shapes of angels that have appeared upon earth, had no other design in so doing, save only the more easily to invite down those blessed spirits by the force of the resemblance. And I know not whether or no, by the very same virtue of resemblance which is found betwixt God and man (*faciamus hominem ad imaginem et similitudinem nostrum*) it hath not rightly been affirmed by some divines, that the Son of God would nevertheless have become man (yet without suffering death) though Adam had never fallen. But speaking of things as they are at present, Jesus Christ is found in the midst of those that speak with faith of his name ; because when we speak (or even *think*) *with affection, of any one, we represent him to ourselves in our imagination* (or in a living *idea*). So true it is that resemblance hath the power to work wonders, even upon him that hath dependence upon no other, and is not under any power or law. But such conceptions as these are to be entertained with all piety, and proposed with such sanctity as becomes those who speak of so adorable a subject."

But the "resemblance" that works the greatest wonders is not a material image that we make to represent the spirit of an angel or a man, but the living image of him that arises in the mind when we interiorly think of him from a true knowledge of him. That image (or idea) is the real man himself, and is invested with all his qualities. It expresses and represents to us not only all that we ever knew of him, but all that he knows and thinks, or ever thought. For what a man *is* in spirit is the sum of all that he ever thought; and when we come into fellowship (or a state of community) with him, through the law of sympathy, his thoughts and feelings, that is, his life, may flow into us. It is all included in his idea or living self. This applies to communion with the manifested God, or the Christ. When we think of God, according to a law of our being, the thought takes form in an idea of him. This idea is God manifested in us, and is really what we are in our inmost nature. It is the Lord coming to personality in man. This vision of the Augoeides, or shining one, as it was called by philosopher initiates, is the revelation of our own inner self as the Lord Christ, and is the Beatific Vision of the "saints." Once enjoyed, its memory never wholly fades from the mind. It is the glorification of our humanity, and the humanization of God as the Lord. Our individual self is not lost in an indefinable "ocean of spirit," but is only enlarged by being incorporated into the Supreme Self. Our little isolated manhood grows into Christhood. And in Christ are hid all the treasures of wisdom and knowledge, and there is no seal on this living book; the seven seals are on men's hearts. When these are broken, and our minds become a peaceful vacancy to the influx of the celestial, the life, light, and love of the Christ flow in and fill the void.

The spirit in man is born of God, and by a law of heredity it inherits the qualities of its parent source. Being begotten in the image and likeness of God, and as a finite limitation of the divine substance, it is immortal in its essence and cannot be diseased or suffer. Of this inward self, Jesus says: "Call no man your father on the earth, for one is your Father, the heavenly." (Matt. xxiii: 9.)

"Never the spirit was born; the spirit shall cease to be never;
Never was time it was not; end and beginning are dreams!
Birthless, and deathless, and changeless remaineth the spirit forever;
Death hath not touched it at all, dead though the house of it seems."
(*The Song Celestial.* Arnold.)

While the spirit is the Son of God, the lower soul is the son of man. In the progress of the evolutionary process the animal soul, or psychical man, is that which first comes into conscious activity, and has a dominating influence over the life. This is called the first man by Paul. The higher man is yet latent, and is the product of a later birth *in* us, the development of a higher region of our being. For "except a man be born from above, he cannot see the kingdom of God" (John iii: 3), but remains blind to it, for the divinest moiety of human nature is unborn in him. The law of the unfoldment of our inner nature is expressed by Paul: "The first man, or Adam, becomes a living soul; the last Adam is a life-giving spirit. Howbeit, that is not first which is spiritual, but that which is natural (or psychical); then that which is spiritual. The first man is of the earth, earthy; the second man is of heaven. And as we have borne the image of the earthy, we shall also bear the image of the heavenly." (1 Cor. xv: 45–49.)

When in the progress of our development the spirit, which

is the celestial man, is born into consciousness, and the inner self is revealed to us, we have found that which can always affirm and speak with authority for every department of our being, "I am not diseased nor unhappy nor sinful, for I and my Father are one." This is that supreme truth, the intuitive knowledge of which makes us free. Such a man, in the grand symbolism of the ancient sages, which in the overwhelming flood of materialism became a dead language to the world, was called an inhabitant of Zion, as mountains signified the celestial state of man on earth. In the descent of the human race from the spiritual to the sensuous and material plane of life it became necessary, in order to preserve the precious and priceless truths of the spirit, to inclose them in symbols addressed to sense. The symbol taken from nature would be as enduring as the pyramids. When, in a subsequent age, men should begin to be unfolded spiritually, the inner content of the symbol would be disclosed. On the development of the intuition in us there is nothing hidden that may not be uncovered to the perception of the spirit. These sublime symbols with their celestial freight, and which men are just beginning to understand, have been an ark borne upon the waters of the flood, which has kept spiritual truth from utter extinction. In this sublime science of correspondence, Zion signifies the celestial or truly spiritual condition of man. And the inhabitant of Zion, or one in whom the recognition of the inner divine self has become an habitual mode of thought, no longer says, "I am sick." (Isa. xxxiii: 24.) For he has discovered the Christ within as the immortal and incorruptible self, which is forever exempt from disease and death. The inward Christ, as the Crown, may say to every one in the language of the king of Persia to Nehemiah, "Why is thy countenance sad, seeing thou art not sick? this is nothing else but sorrow of heart." (Neh. ii: 2.) And this sorrow, or mental inharmony which the world calls disease, is only in the sensuous mind, a region of being that is far below the summit of Zion, the residence of the true self. Here man ceases from desire and finds rest. The unsatisfied desires of the selfish animal soul engender sorrow and pain and disease. This inward turbulence and disquiet translate themselves into a bodily expression. But when we discover the Christ within, we have quenched this *trishna*, or burning thirst, from springs that never dry.

> "Then all the jarring notes of life
> Seem blending in a psalm,
> And all the angles of its strife
> Slow rounding into calm."

"The ransomed of the Lord *return* and come with singing unto Zion; everlasting joy shall be upon their heads; they shall obtain gladness and joy, and sorrow and sighing shall flee away." (Isa. xxxv: 10.)

You will perceive, from the wording of the above beautiful passage, that the attainment of a state where sorrow and sighing, or that dissatisfied condition of the soul which is the essence of mental disease, shall flee away, and fall off from the inward man like raindrops from the leaves in a summer shower, is not a new creation in us, but a *return* to a state from which we have descended. It is a mistake to suppose that the life of the spirit, the real and immortal *Ego*, is measured by the brief span of a few revolving years on earth. According to the oldest spiritual philosophy, which has come down from an age when the "sun of righteousness" shone upon men without being obscured by the clouds of sense, our life here is but the bottom segment of a cycle or circle of existence. The life on earth, with its mixed joys and sorrows, pleasures and pains, is the lowest portion of the cycle. It is an adumbration and an eclipse of "that glory which we had with the Father before the world was" to us. Life here is at the furthest remove from its Divine Source.

And our progressive regeneration is, in fact, the homeward-bound journey of the soul. As a planet when it reaches its aphelion, or point of greatest remoteness from the sun, in its elliptical orbit, begins to come back to its perihelion, or place of greatest nearness to the central and luminous world around which it revolves, so we commence our *return* to the realm of pure spirit (which is symbolically called Zion) when we discover and lament our remoteness from the Deific Centre of all existence, and the region that is the true home of our souls. Life is a stream which has its rise in the Mount of God, and the further it flows from its source, the more turbid its waters become. When we discover this great truth, and say, " I will arise and go to my Father," and turn about (which in the terminology of the New Testament is called *conversion*), the stream of our life is reversed, and begins to flow back towards its origin. To find the spiritual state for which we inwardly yearn, we are not to look forward and explore an unknown and unknowable future, for it is not there. We look in the wrong direction. However sharply we scrutinize the future, we shall miss the object of quest. We have already gone far enough in that direction. By an introversion of the mind we are to look back, and recover into consciousness our former spiritual state and pristine glory by *recollection*. In the inverted state of our powers and perceptions, what we call progress is really a return. This is the teaching of Plato, and also of Jesus. Retrogression is the true advance. We believe this is a principle of supreme practical value, and shall return to it again in the following pages. Great prominence was given to that introversion of mind, or turning of the mind inward upon itself, which was called recollection, by the mystics of the Middle Ages, who were only Christian Platonists. They did not seek to invent or create truth, but to recover it by memory. On an examination of a concordance of the Scriptures under the word remember and its derivatives, we shall be astonished to find how great a prominence was given to the memory in the evolution of the spiritual life, a principle which has been ignored in modern times. In the spirit of the old philosophy, we would say, "Remember, therefore, from whence thou art fallen, and repent and do the first works." (Rev. ii : 5.)

CHAPTER VIII.

THE BREATH OF GOD IN MAN, OR THE TRUE ELIXIR OF LIFE.

THE "Unknown," the Divine Esse, or Absolute Being, has let himself down from his inscrutable height which cannot be scaled by finite thought, by three degrees of manifestation, and each successive stage of the revelation of himself is in itself, and taken by itself, a triad of principles, or a trinity in unity. The third is the Universal Life, a Divine Principle or primordial substance (not in a material, but in a metaphysical sense). This is God as the intelligent Life of the world, and is called Adonai, or Lord. It may be viewed in thought, if you choose, as a person, for in the Oriental mind everything is personified. It is identical with the Holy Spirit of the New Testament. It is the ultimate expression of the Christ or Manifested God. In the Kabala, the divine name which corresponds to the tenth Sephira, or emanative principle, and which represents the whole realm of actuality (or matter) is Adonai, who is the everywhere present and all-intelligent life-force in nature. In the grand economy of existence, or the manifestation of being, it is the function of this demiurgic, or world-building intellect, to translate pre-existing subjective ideas into actuality, or objective forms and material representations. This will render clear all that we may say hereafter.

There are certain plants which live wholly from the air, and all plants do so more or less, as a geranium placed under the exhausted receiver of an air-pump will die. Every vital process is instantly suspended. Now air is the correspondent of the Holy Spirit. Wind, which is air in motion, or as force, is the representation of Spirit in action. Hence Jesus says, "The Spirit bloweth (or breatheth) where it listeth, and thou hearest the sound of it, but canst not tell whence it cometh, nor whither it goeth. So is every one who is born of the Spirit. (John iii : 8.) As plants live mostly from the air, since their several tissues are but a condensation or crystallization (as it were) of the four principal gases, may not man as a physical being live from the Holy Spirit, the universal living energy and principle of life? All men do in fact so live, but may we not have this life more abundantly?

There is a Universal Life Principle, which is the intelligent, animating force of the world and of the human body. It is in all things, and all things are in it. It has been recognized and worshipped under different names by the various nations of men in all ages, as a manifestation of God. Among the Greeks it was called Zeus (from ζάω, to live) and was identical with the Universal Æther, eliminating from the word all material conceptions. Cicero speaks of Zeus as *pater omnipotens Æther*. Among the Hindus it is denominated *Akasa*, a reduplication of the word for life, and was the god-sky, not the visible, but invisible sky, and was considered by them as an everywhere present vivific principle and primal force. As the divine, operating presence of God in the world and in man, it is called Adonai or Lord in the Old Testament. It is the *anima mundi* of Pythagoras and Plato, or the world-soul, sustaining to the material universe the same relation that the animal soul of man does to the human body. To learn how to invigorate, augment, and reinforce our individual and particular life from the Universal Life, our soul from the Universal Soul, is to find the true Elixir Vitæ, one of the objects of quest among the Alchemists. Is it an impossible attainment? Swedenborg affirms and reiterates the assertion, that there is but one Life among angels and men, and that Life is the Lord, and that man is so made that he can appropriate to himself life from the Lord. We may live and grow as the flower imbibes the vivifying light and heat of the sun. The white lotus on the still lagoon, when the sun sets, contracts its stem and draws itself under water, as does our beautiful *Nymphœa Odorata*. When the sun rises, it comes to the surface, expands its closed petals, and opens itself to receive the solar light and life. Let us behold the lilies of the field, how they grow, and imitate them. The selfhood or *proprium* of man, that which we call our own, is only a capacity, a capability of receiving, a subjective possibility of existence. The divinely intelligent world-soul — call it the Lord, the *Akasa*, the Holy Spirit, or by whatever name you please to give it, or let it be nameless, — is always inclined to heal the hurts of every living thing. We have a favorite dog who received a severe gun-shot wound. For two days he lay as if asleep. He did nothing, and nothing was done for him. In three days he had recovered. Who cured the dog? A valuable cherry-tree on our grounds was badly injured by a fractious horse backing a loaded wagon against it. A cotton bandage was placed over the wound by one of our patients. In a year it was removed, and the wound was healed. Who healed the tree? A mussel with one valve accidentally broken into a dozen fragments was returned to his sandy bed on the banks of the Merrimac, and in a brief time the shell was artistically mended; the wound was healed with no signs of the injury left but the scars. Who and what healed the clam? He only lay still in the sand, and was healed by him who feeds the young ravens when they cry, and cares for the sparrows, and who perpetually endeavors to realize the Divine idea of things in nature. It is a divine essence and can never be diseased or die; only its manifestations can be disorderly.

As an ultimate expression of the life of the Christ, it healeth all our diseases, and redeemeth our life from destruction, so that our youth is renewed like the eagle's. (Ps. ciii: 1–5.)

The reception of this animating and saving principle is by influx according to a law of correspondence, as the Hermetic philosophers of all lands have received knowledge. As God and nature abhor a vacuum, if we approach the Lord of life in a spirit of emptiness or true spiritual poverty, he will fill our needs from his illimitable fulness. The most effectual prayer is wordless — the turning of a soul, conscious of its emptiness towards the boundless Life of the heavens and of nature. For there is but one Lord, and the same Lord is the Lord of all, and is rich unto all that call upon him, whether it be the wounded animal whose passive silence is as eloquent as the strains of an archangel, or the ejaculation of the humble publican outside of the temple. (Rom. x: 12.) Man's life is not self-originated or generated within the limits of his physical organism, but is perpetually imparted from the Lord. There is but one Life, one Love, one Intelligence, and one Power or Force. All finite, individual life is a manifestation of the one Life; all love is an exhibition of the supreme Love; all intelligence, in plants, animals, men, and angels is a ray of the infinite Intelligence; and all strength is an expression of the one Force, for all power is of God. (Rom. xiii: 1.) Disease is a state of weakness, an infirmity, because it is a condition where by a wrong way of thinking we come into a feeling of isolation from the Lord; but "blessed (or happy) is the man whose strength is in thee." (Ps. lxxxiv: 5.) Strength is a purely mental state and mental energy, as much so as faith and hope. We are to banish from our minds the deeply rooted illusion of physical strength and bodily weakness. The mental force that we call strength can be received by influx from the Lord. "They that wait upon the Lord shall renew their strength." (Isa. xl: 31.)

In the Old Testament Scriptures one of the designations of the universal Life-Principle, or the Holy Spirit, is "the breath of God." In Paul's oration before the Areopagus he affirms that the nameless Deity to whose worship he found an altar dedicated in Athens, and who is not far from every one of us, is he who giveth life and breath and all things. (Acts xvii: 25.) The same forgotten truth is taught in that ancient mystic poem, the Book of Job. In speaking of the Supreme Being he says: "In whose hand is the soul of every living thing, and the breath of all mankind." (Job xii: 10.) Again, "The Spirit of God hath made me, and the breath of the Almighty hath given me life." (Job xxx: 4.) In another place he says, "By the breath of God frost is given." (Job xxxvii: 10.) We are to bear in mind that the Universal Life-Principle is called in the Scriptures the breath of God. And every frost crystal, with its intelligent geometrical forms, with the angles made by its rays all exactly of sixty degrees, is the result of the action of an everywhere present, living energy, as much so as all the myriad forms of vegetable and animal organization. All phenomena are the expression of life. *By our breathing we are connected with the Universal Life-Principle. At that point my particular life meets and mingles with the One Life.* This gives an importance to respiration that few have noticed. As Dr. Wilkinson has eloquently said, "In the running wheel of life the imperceptible motion at the axle is thought; the sweep at the periphery is respiration." (*The Human Body and its Connection with Man*, p. 59.) Right *thinking* and right *breathing* are the two things most essential to happiness and health. Our modes of thought and feeling are ultimated in the body through the respiration. Every mental state has a respiration answering to it. Take as an illustration the mental act of listening to catch a faint and distant sound. It suspends the breathing. You cannot listen and breathe deep and full. The instant you do this, you stop listening. The same is true of melancholy. It stops the machinery of life by suspending the respiration. So of all our varying mental states. They record themselves on the Universal Life-Principle, and through this in a respiratory movement peculiar to them. Tell a young lad that he cannot lift a rock that lies before him, and if he accepts your challenge, he instinctively assumes an erect attitude, the posture of the "upright" man, takes a full breath, and triumphantly raises the rock. There is a practical and profound philosophy in what he does. He first forms the *idea* of strength. He then ultimates it in a bodily attitude, and translates the idea into a form of respiration that belongs to it, and through this it becomes a vigorous muscular contraction. In a similar way, any desirable mental state of which we can form an *idea* may be ultimated in the life. The first act of conscious life was respiration, and it will be the last. All our sense-consciousness commenced with it, and is coeval and coexistent with it throughout the whole cycle of our earthly existence. As Mrs. Browning has said, "He lives most life whoever breathes most air."

But we ask, What is the connection of our respiration with the Universal Life-Principle, called the breath of God? In answering this query, we remark that all motion in the universe is rhythmical, as Herbert Spencer has shown in his *First Principles of Philosophy*. This is seen in the forward and backward movement of the pendulum, the ebb and flow of the tides, the succession of day and night, the systolic and diastolic action of the heart, and in the inspiration and expiration of the lungs. Our breathing is a double motion of the universal æther, an active and a reactive movement.

This androgyne principle, with its dual motion, is the breath of life, the breath of God in man. When we breathe in harmony with this movement, we are well, and our individual life marches forward in exact step with the tranquil life of nature; when our respiration is discordant with it, our life-force is out of tune. We are a discord in the divine song of creation. Says Herbert Spencer in the *Popular Science Monthly* for January, 1884: "Amid the mysteries that become the more mysterious the more they are thought about, there will remain the one absolute certainty, that we are ever in the presence of an infinite and an eternal energy, from which all things proceed." With this grand confession of faith, he takes his place in the ranks of an ever-growing number of scientific theists. The Universal Æther of the Hermetic philosophy, the Adonai of the Kabala, the Holy Spirit, the *Anima Mundi*, the *Welt-geist*, is an infinite, eternal, and living and life-giving energy, in the midst of which we ever are, and from whose presence we can never escape. (Ps. cxxxix: 7–10.) And it is its presence which is a never-ceasing outgoing from God, with its self-moving dual action, and *double motion*, that gives the breath of life. It breathes in and for us when we retire from the physiological machine, as in sleep, and whenever our breathing is automatic and involuntary. Then our respiratory movements arise out of that mysterious, universal, and eternal (but to materialistic science inexplicable) vital impulse that lies at the root of all the manifestations of life in the universe. The nearer we can assume toward it in our wakeful hours the passive attitude of sleep, as in the case of the wounded dog mentioned above, the more it can and will do for us. We need to learn the lesson of trust so beautifully expressed by Whittier.

"Rocked on her breast, these pines and I
Alike on Nature's love rely;
And equal seems to live or die,

> "Assured that he whose presence fills
> With light the spaces of these hills
> No evil to his creatures wills,
>
> "The simple faith remains, that He
> Will do, whatever that may be,
> The best alike for man and tree.
>
> What mosses over one shall grow,
> What light and life the other know,
> Unanxious, leaving Him to show."

The action of this universal curative principle may be modified by the will, faith, and imagination of man, and its operation accelerated in the divine curative or saving process. The Holy Spirit of the New Testament is a "divine proceeding," as Swedenborg denominates it; or, in other words, an emanative principle from God, and one which is the operative energy of God in nature and in man. Among other manifestations of its presence and agency, it is that which is the principle of respiration, and this movement thus springs out of the universal Life. It is, as we have before said, the primary movement, and that from which all others arise and on which they depend. It modifies and controls all the other physiological movements. Paul affirms that our body is a temple of the Holy Spirit, which is in us, and which we have from God. Therefore we should glorify God (or think rightly of him) *in* our body. (1 Cor. vi: 19, 20.) As the Holy Spirit is the only life of our body, it surely ought not to be difficult to think that it is never sick or sinful. We may be affected by the "world," or that current of thought and feeling in society around us, which is the antagonist of the true spiritual life.

But the Holy Spirit is what Jesus denominates it, $\tau\grave{o}\ \pi\nu\epsilon\hat{v}\mu\alpha\ \tau\grave{o}\ \ \ddot{\alpha}\gamma\iota\text{ov}$, the unearthly spirit, or the purely divine life-principle uncontaminated by the disorderly life of the world. It is that by which and in which God is present in the world and in man. It is also that medium or vehicle through which and in which the risen and glorified Jesus can come to his disciples or scholars. It is *the principle of presence* of one spirit with another. Through it Jesus comes to his true followers as the *Lord Christ*, the Master or Teacher divinely illuminated, the Paraclete or spirit of truth, to teach us all things, to guide us into all truth, and recall forgotten spiritual verities to our recollection. (John xiv : 26.) It is a mistake to suppose that Jesus has ever left the world. He declared to his disciples, " I will not leave you desolate (or orphans) ; I come to you." (John xiv : 18.) " Lo, I am with you always, even unto the consummation of the age." (Matt. xxviii : 20.) In his ascension to the purely spiritual plane of life, a cloud received him out of sight; but the cloud was not in the upper atmosphere, but was a cloud of sensuality in the minds of men. He disappeared from vision by the closure of the inner senses of men. And this same Jesus, whom we have thus seen go into heaven, shall in like manner return as we have seen him go into heaven. (Acts i : 9–11.) He disappeared from men by the closing of their spiritual vision. He comes to men by the rending of the veil of sense and the opening of the eyes of the understanding. In our mental and physical maladies there is help at hand, for Jesus who is not far off in the immeasurable depths of space, but still in the world he loves, comes to men to breathe into them the quickening spirit. And through the everywhere present medium of the Universal Life, the Holy Spirit, saving truth may be communicated by him, and healing impressions may be fastened upon the minds of men, as easily and as naturally as an electric force is conveyed through the wire, or a sound impulse through the telephone. Psychological effects can be produced, and thoughts and ideas communicated from mind to mind, in this world or the realm above, without the intervention of any material apparatus or conducting wires, by thought infused into and impressed upon the invisible world-spirit, the Divine Æther.

The Holy Spirit is the *I Am* of our soul-life and physical force. In and of itself it is (so to speak) a formless *substance* of life. It is for us to *name* it, and the name we give it, it takes, and in that quality we may appropriate it and *breathe it in*. The very word for soul (*psyche*) comes from a Greek verb meaning to breathe. For by our breath we are connected with the universal life-principle, and our soul is a finite limitation of it. But it takes quality from our fixed modes of thought and confirmed beliefs. If these are illusions, and the acceptance as realities of false appearances, the physical organism will become their outward expression. If we form the true idea of ourself, and tranquilly hold to it, the Holy Spirit will translate the divine idea into a bodily representation; for as we have before said, the office of the Holy Spirit is to give material form and actuality to subjective ideas.

The Holy Spirit is the medium or vehicle through which spiritual blessings come to us from the "Father," and from the highest realm of existence. The promise is, "Ask, and it shall be given"; and what we ask, which is an aspiration or breathing out of the soul into the all-surrounding Life, is returned to us as an inspiration or inbreathing. That of which we form a conception and which we *desire*, becomes a reality, a living thing in the universal life-principle, one of the occult properties of which is *reaction*, and what we thus ask is reflected back to us somewhat as a sound is returned in an echo through the æther, which is the medium of the transmission of sound; or as an empty bucket comes back from the well, filled with water, which takes the form of the vessel that contains it. Thus as Jesus teaches in the Gospel of Luke the Essene, "If a child ask bread, his father does not give him a stone; or if he asks for a fish, he does not give him a serpent; or if he asks for an egg, he does not give him a scorpion. If we then being evil know how to give good gifts to our children, how much more shall our heavenly Father give the Holy Spirit to them that ask him." (Luke xi: 9–13.) And it will take the form, or quality, that is the object of thought and desire in the request, and this by a profound law of our being. The Holy Spirit is a universal Proteus, which like that marine deity, or divine principle in nature, has the property of taking the shape of our desires and thoughts. True prayer is aspiration, or the soul breathing after a thing, and its answer is an inbreathing, as the nursing of a child is only a modified respiration. This universal divine Soul of the Universe is to us what we make it by our confirmed mode of thinking and believing. The highest ideal that we can form of existence on earth is the perpetual vigor of youth combined with the wisdom of age. Whatever is conceivable by the mind of man is *possible*. The first step towards the realization of that divine idea of man is the conception (or begetting) of it in our minds and the belief of its attainableness. We then remove it from the category of impossible things, and plant the living seed of it in our souls, and the Holy Spirit will preside over its development into actuality in ourselves and others. For we affirm again, it is the function of the Holy Spirit to give an ultimate or material expression to divine ideas. If there was on earth among men a higher *idea* of man, we should have a higher race of men.

The question was put to Jesus by those who witnessed his marvellous cures, "What must we do that we may work the works of God?" His reply, when fully comprehended, solves the mystery of a true theurgy, and reveals one of the fundamental principles of the ancient occult spiritual philosophy in its application to the cure of the sick and sinful by psychological impression. "This is the work of God, that ye believe on that which he hath sent." (John vi: 28, 29.) By the *sent* of God is not signified any mere historic person, but that which emanates or proceeds from God, and which is his representative in nature, and that which manifests him in the world. He who would work the works of God, or do the things that lie beyond the common doings of men, must say in the language of the Apostle's creed, but with a deeper meaning than is usually given to the words, " I believe in the Holy Ghost"; not merely in the teaching of the popular theology in regard to him, but as possessing a fuller knowledge of his nature and functions. This divine life and force in nature comes to the aid of him who can think and act on the spiritual plane of his being. He who fully *believes* in it, comes to an interior cognition of it, and becomes one with it. It is a "Spirit of truth," which the world cannot receive, because it seeth it not by the senses, neither knoweth it. "But ye know him," says Jesus to his disciples, "for he dwelleth with you and shall be *in* you." (John xiv: 17.) If we come into sympathy with the life of nature and its Universal Soul, we can, by the power of our minds when acting above the plane of sense, intensify its saving energy, and direct it to the cure of disease. Jesus sent the Holy Spirit in his *name*, or in the healing quality and virtue which the sphere of his life gave to it, and which is signified by his name. Is it not possible for us in this day to do, in some measure at least, what he did? He says, in immediate connection with this subject, "Verily, verily, I say unto you, he that believeth on me, the works that I do shall he do also; and greater works than these shall he do; because I go unto my Father." (John xiv: 12.) In the apostolic age the Holy Spirit was communicated by the imposition of the hands. It is a doctrine of Christianity that has been buried out of sight by the Church beneath its accumulated theological rubbish, and the debris of the primitive system, that when a man is in a state of spiritual impletion, or is surcharged with the life, light, and power of the Spirit, he may impart it to others as a divine illuminating and healing virtue. This may be done by the power of the right word, by a psychological impression and thought impulse, by a strong will and determined imagination, and by the imposition of the hands. (See Acts viii : 14-24; xix : 1-7.) When we have accumulated the divine life of nature into ourselves, and possess it in an overflowing fulness, our surplusage of spiritual life and mental healthfulness is given us to be imparted to others to supply their lack and fill their emptiness, just as a thousand smoking wicks may be lighted from one well-trimmed and well-filled lamp without diminishing its own flame. There are thousands of invalids who need this, and are saying in their hearts, if not with their lips, " Give us of your oil, for our torches are going out." By communicating to them the Holy Spirit, we put them in contact with the Universal Life, where they may buy for themselves, and thus become divinely self-reliant. The Holy Spirit, as an emanation from God, is the true Bethesda and pool of Siloam, which is by interpretation, the Sent. Whoever steps into this pool is healed of whatsoever disease he has.

In the earlier and purer philosophy of Buddhism it was taught that the *Akasa* contained a permanent record of all that was ever thought, *felt*, said, or done. These are all preserved in that universal principle as in " a book of life," or living book. All our states of thought and emotion exist in it, and can never have existence outside of it. There is in man a potential capacity to read the record. What we call memory is the recalling into consciousness of things that are connected with our personal existence. On the development of the intuition in us we can read the general record, and man is capable of knowing all that was ever known, and of feeling all that was ever felt. Education was supposed to be what the word radically signifies, the recalling of truths and states that belonged to a former and higher existence of man. Such was the doctrine of Plato. However that may be, all our higher and better experiences from infancy to age have a present existence in the *Akasa*; or, to use the term employed by Jesus, in the Holy Spirit, and through this medium may be revived into present consciousness in us. The Holy Spirit is given to call all things to our remembrance that Jesus has said to the world. (John xiv: 26.) Forgotten truths are again revealed to us. So all our past joys and peaceful states, and youthful innocence, strength, and bliss, still exist in the universal life, and through the Holy Spirit may be revived into a present conscious perception. Memory exists only in this universal divine principle, and has a deeper and wider significance than is usually given to it in our modern systems of philosophy. It is the golden link which unites the past with the present and the future. The Holy Spirit is the ark that carries all sacred truths and good affections across the flood from the past into the eternal now. The happy emotions and innocent joys of childhood are not lost out of the general Life, nor out of our individual being. Youthfulness, which is only *adolescence* or intellectual and spiritual *growth*, is not an irrecoverable state. Perpetual youth is a conceivable and consequently a possible condition. As our spirit is included in the Christ, and is complete in him who is the head of all principality and power, so also our soul-life, with all its happy emotions, past and present, is preserved to us in the Holy Spirit. All that we ever enjoyed may come back to us, and with increase. Nothing that is good and true ever perishes; the evil and the false, not having the divine life in them, are evanescent. They are blotted out from the book of the living memory. The excellent is alone the permanent. That which is not, never will be; that which really is, will never cease to be. Our youthful states of healthful vigor, and the blessedness of our early life, which sometimes gleam transiently into our consciousness, like a star looking from behind a cloud, are not annihilated. They are like flowers that close at night. When the sun of righteousness arises within us, they will open again.

> "On the heaven heights of Truth
> The true soul keeps its youth."

In all the darkness, trials, sorrows, and diseases of life it may be made certain to our faith that our joys, and the blessedness of former days, are not lost out of our inner being. They are there as a priceless remnant that the Universal Life has treasured up and will restore. (Isa. i: 9.) When the Lord turns our captivity, and we emerge from our states of vastation and trial, and the deaths and hells through which the way to "glory" sometimes lies, the experience of Job may be ours. The Lord gave to Job twice as much as he had before, and his latter days were more blessed than the beginning. (Job xlii: 10–12.)

The ancient poem, called the Book of Job, is not historical; but in it is given under symbolic representations the inner history of the soul, its pristine glory and descent into matter, and its return to its first estate. The latter day of prosperity, with its multiplied possessions, was only the coming round and development into conscious recollection of a former state of existence, with all the additions of good and truth which had been gathered up into the soul's life by its subsequent experiences. The "wheel of life" in its revolution had returned the soul to the spiritual state whence it had started, and it had carried back with it the results of all the temptations and trials of its earthly existence. The same great spiritual law is stated by Paul, when he says: "Our light affliction, which is for the moment, worketh for us more and more exceedingly an eternal weight of glory, while we look not at the things which are seen, but at the things which are not seen (by sense); for the things which are seen are temporal; but the things which are not seen are eternal." (1 Cor. iv: 17, 18.) In the original we have one of the strongest expressions in human language to give us a conception of that increment of good that comes to the soul as the result of the trials of its earth-life, and one which it is impossible to translate without a circumlocution. For "more and more exceedingly" we have, in the Greek καθ' ὑπερβολὴν εἰς ὑπερβολήν, — with hyperbole upon hyperbole. The figure of speech, called in rhetoric an hyperbole, is an extravagant exaggeration, as when we speak of a flood of tears. But, according to Paul, we may place hyperbole upon hyperbole, like Pelium upon Ossa, and Ossa upon Olympus, and you fail to measure and weigh by words that weight of glory (or spiritual illumination and enduring good) which will result from the trials of our earthly existence. What we mourn as the evils of our lot, influenced in our judgment by the illusions of sense, are our highest inheritance of good. The tears we sow will spring up and mature into a golden harvest, which in due time we shall reap and garner up among our eternal treasures. When we can see through the opening clouds of sense the glimmering light of these great truths, we shall no longer call good evil, nor evil, good. Then

> "Life's burdens fall, its discords cease,
> I lapse into the glad release
> Of Nature's own exceeding peace.
>
> "O, welcome calm of heart and mind!
> As falls yon fir-tree's loosened rind
> To leave a tenderer growth behind,
>
> "So fall the weary years away:
> A child again, my head I lay
> Upon the lap of this sweet day."

CHAPTER IX.

PAIN AND ITS MENTAL CONQUEST.

It appears from the sayings of Jesus, that he possessed the keys of death and Hades, or that he had attained to a perfect control of the life of the body, so that death was a voluntary surrender on his part, and not a conquest. He says: "Therefore does my Father love me, because I lay down (or give up) my life, that I may take it again. No one taketh it away from me, but I lay it down myself. I have power to lay it down, and I have power to take it again. This commandment (or instruction) received I from my Father." (John x: 17, 18.) To some extent, at least, if not in the fulness of the power possessed by Jesus, it is an attainable condition—far more so than the world at large has been educated to believe. There have been men in the world who have possessed the control of the life of the body to such a degree that they lived as long as they desired to live. Death had no more a dominion over them, for they were not under law, that is, the controlling influence of public opinion, but under grace, or the hidden spiritual wisdom. (Rom. vi: 8–14.) This control of the life of the body was one of the objects of quest by the Alchemists, and it is believed that some of them attained to it. And there are intelligent people who believe that there are to-day men on earth, the years of whose life are very far from being bounded by a single century. In reference to this we neither affirm nor deny. Before we wholly reject it as absurd, incredible, and impossible, we do well to pause and ask, Is it in harmony with the teaching of Jesus and of Christianity? Is man's present condition the utmost limit of his powers? Has human nature attained to its full spiritual growth? If there are any unevolved possibilities in man, then we may rise to and bring forth something higher. A brief half-century ago few would have deemed it possible that two men could intelligibly communicate with each other across the Atlantic Ocean, or talk with each other a hundred miles apart, for such an achievement would have been considered as impossible as to fly to the moon.

Life is manifested on three distinct or discrete planes of existence; and the higher, in accordance with the divine order, may govern the lower. It is a law of our being, established and perpetuated by an everywhere present Deity, that spirit should dominate all the physical functions. Jesus affirms, "He that liveth and believeth in me shall never die." (John xi: 26.) Again, "He who believeth on the Son (which includes our own inward divine spirit) hath everlasting life," as a present attainment. (John iii: 16.) These and similar passages manifestly mean more than the popular religion of the day finds in them. It is predicted by the best of the Jewish prophets that in the Messianic age that was to be born, the life of man would be greatly prolonged, "for as the days of a tree shall be the days of my people." (Isa. lxv: 20-22.) But it is our purpose to speak more particularly of pain and its mental remedy.

In that higher condition of man, which is called the new heavens and the new earth, and which is nothing but the attainment of a truly spiritual and celestial state, and its ultimate expression in the body, it is said there shall be no more pain. (Rev. xxi: 4.) Pain and disease are the result of the fall of man, or the lapse of humanity from the plane of the spiritual life to a state of bondage to matter and the lower senses; and the cure must consist in the surrender of the lower animal soul to the rightful dominion of the spirit, the Christ within, who must be allowed to reign in us until every enemy is put under his feet; and the last enemy that shall be destroyed is death. When we attain the true Christian position of thought, and death becomes transformed into resurrection, or the ascent of the soul to a new and higher life on earth, then pain and disease disappear from consciousness. The soul is, as it were, separated from the body; that is, it is freed from the limitations of matter and released from its corporeal dungeon. When the Christ within us, the immortal and divine spirit in us, sheds its living radiance upon all the lower or outer departments of our being, then the immortal life animates our clay, and the vivifying breath of God moves the physiological machinery in harmony with all that is divine in nature. This is the coming of the Christ in the flesh, and in our flesh. It is the Lord, the One Life, and "one thing needful," coming to his temple, a purified human body, and coming the prisoner to release long held in the bondage of matter, and to open the prison to all that within us which is bound. It is the advent of the Logos, the inner and living Word, the true light that lighteth every man that cometh into the world, and this light is the life of man; and this Word is made flesh, or is ultimated in a bodily expression in harmony with it, and dwells *in* us, which is the true rendering, not among us, as if it was something outside of us and foreign to our true being. (John i: 14.) In this resurrection day, the real man, the immortal self, comes forth from the sepulchre of the body, and lives eternal life while on earth.

The various anæsthetics afford insensibility to the pains of disease and of surgical operations, by temporarily releasing the soul from the body, a condition of existence which is attainable as a philosophical and religious state without the use of drugs, as the Hindu *Soma* drink, or the more modern nitrous oxide. Says Sir Humphry Davy, the English chemist, in describing his sensations after inhaling the gas:

"I began to respire twenty quarts of unmingled nitrous oxide. A thrilling extending from the chest to the extremities was almost immediately produced. I felt a sense of tangible extension highly pleasurable in every limb; my visible impressions were dazzling, and apparently magnified; I heard distinctly every sound in the room, and was perfectly aware of my situation. By degrees, as the pleasurable sensations increased, I lost all connection with external things; trains of vivid visible images rapidly passed through my mind, and were connected with words in such a manner as to produce perceptions perfectly novel. I existed in a world of newly-connected and newly-modified ideas. I theorized, I imagined that I made discoveries. When I was awakened from this semi-delirious trance by Dr. Kinglake, who took the bag from my mouth, indignation and pride were the first feelings produced by the sight of the persons about me. My emotions were enthusiastic and sublime; and for a minute I walked around the room, perfectly regardless of what was said to me. As I recovered my former state of mind I felt an inclination to communicate the discoveries I had made during the experiment. I endeavored to recall the ideas; they were feeble and indistinct; one collection of terms, however, presented itself; and with the most intense belief and prophetic manner, I exclaimed to Dr. Kinglake, '*Nothing exists but thoughts! The universe is composed of impressions, ideas, pleasures, and pains!*' About three minutes and a half only had elapsed during this experiment, though the time, as measured by the relative vividness of the collected ideas, appeared to me much longer."

This emancipation of the soul from the limitations of the body, and the bondage of the inner man to the external senses, which gives us the mastery of pain and disease, effected in an abnormal way by the use of anæsthetics, and which transformed the materialistic scientist and chemist into an idealistic philosopher temporarily, is a state into which mankind can be educated or developed. It is among the unevolved potentialities of our nature. It is a permanent, religious, and philosophical state which has been realized in the experience of the few, who have appeared occasionally along the path of human history as pioneers and heralds of a better day for the world. They are signals sparsely set along the battlements of heaven, flashing into the solid darkness of the world the good news, "the kingdom of the heavens is at hand." This state of emancipation from the body, and the deceptive and erroneous appearances and illusions of the senses, is the same as the Neo-Platonic ecstasy, which was deemed necessary to the attainment of the highest philosophical and spiritual altitude of thought and life. Our bondage to the animal senses, which is the taste of that forbidden tree that brought death and disease and pain and all our woe into the world, is an inverted, unnatural — and may we not say, ungodly? — condition. And who shall deliver us from "the body of this death"? In the language of Paul, who found the way, "I thank God, through our Lord Jesus Christ," who is within us as the hidden centre of our being. Pain and disease are not necessities of our earthly existence. There is a way out. He who has found the Christ within, his own immortal spirit, an emanation from the supreme and universal Spirit, and which partakes of all the attributes and perfections of its parent Source, can say: "I am the first and the last, and the One who lives; and I was dead, and behold I am alive for evermore, and I have the keys of death and Hades," to open the door and walk out into God's great sunlight. (Rev. i : 17, 18.) The present movement of the public mind in the direction of the cure of disease and sin (in the Platonic sense of an error of the understanding) must be received by all thinking people as one of the most important movements in philosophy and religion which modern history has been called upon to record. It is the first feeble shaking of the dry bones of the past Golden Age of the world, buried beneath the sensuous materialistic science of modern times, and which is now struggling into a resurrection. I discover in it the pulse-beats of a higher life in humanity. Like primitive Christianity, there will be much that will try to fasten itself upon it that has no vital connection with it, and it will be opposed by the modern scribes, or "letter-men" of the law, and by a narrow, Pharisaic bigotry, and even Herod may seek to slay the young child, but nevertheless the infant is fully born, like Minerva or wisdom, from the brain of Jupiter, and the child will increase in wisdom and stature, and in favor with God and men. But let us bear in mind that the movement, if it signifies anything of a permanent value to the world, means a higher development of the spiritual life of man. It is only in this way that we can ever hope to attain to the mastery of pain and disease by the mind (or thinking principle), in the dethronement of the bodily senses, and the establishment of the empire of the spirit in us, whose kingdom is an everlasting kingdom, and all other dominions must serve and obey it. The overthrow of the "fourth kingdom" of Daniel, the "iron age" of Greek and Roman mythology, and which marks the reign in us of materialism and sensualism in religion and science, is accomplished by the "mystic stone" cut without hands from the mountain, — the symbol of the celestial degree of life, — and which is identical with the "white stone" of the Apocalypse, and the "philosopher's stone" of the Alchemists, and this, as Trithemius affirms, is none other than our own immortal and divine spirit. In the language of Paul, when correctly rendered, "Great is the mystery of godliness which is manifested in the flesh." (1 Tim. iii: 16.)

In an old definition of pain, which dates as far back as Aristotle, and which has been reproduced by Sir William

Hamilton, and adopted into his metaphysical system, we have a hint for the application of what will prove in very many cases an infallible remedy for it, and one of which we should never lose sight. It is a remedy we shall have frequent occasion to prescribe for ourselves and others. Says Hamilton: "Pleasure is a reflex (that is, effect, result) of the spontaneous and unimpeded exertion of a power of which we are conscious; pain, a reflex of the overstrained or *repressed* exertion of such a power." (*Lectures on Metaphysics*, p. 577.) Here is a golden truth of great practical value. If we substitute for pleasure and pain the words health and disease, it is equally true. Most diseases and painful affections, so far as they have become a condition of the physical organism, are a *stasis* or standing still of the circulation both of the blood and of the soul-principle through the parts. To put any organ, or muscle, as an arm or a leg, to its legitimate (not overstrained) use, is always pleasurable and healthful. Most diseases are the result of a repressed or obstructed activity of some part of the body. To find out the divinest use of any power of mind or body, and to put it to that use, is the law of its health and the sovereign remedy for its disease. Take as an illustration, the lameness and soreness of the muscles of the arm, especially the Deltoid muscle, whose office is to raise the arm. The pain here is only a crying out of the part for more blood, more soul-life. Each successive time the arm is slowly raised, the pain is less and less, until at length it wholly disappears. The same is true of that most painful disease, acute or chronic inflammation of the sciatic nerve, or the ordinary forms of rheumatism. In the former case, the sciatic nerve, one of the largest in the body, has become "strangulated," as some medical author expresses it. It cries out for more of the soul-life in it. Gently move it a few times, and then, "Arise, take up thy bed, and walk."

Soreness and pain in a part of the body, to speak after the manner of men, are only the same thing in different degrees, — a want of life in the part. And the voluntary movement of a part determines the vital force to the part moved. A weak muscle is always sore. Action is the law of life, and consequently of health. Inaction is first pain, and then death. He who fully comprehends this principle, and can bring the patient to a practical application of it, will be a successful physician; for the cure of disease is only the restoration of the organs involved in it to their legitimate functional use and activity. During the last quarter of a century, by an application of this principle, I have wrought many "miracles" (in the popular estimation), and a large proportion of the marvels of healing, witnessed at the present time, are illustrations of the principle we are discussing in this article. The better way is to educate the patient into the application of this principle, and then he works his own "miracles," and in a spirit of self-reliance, becomes his own *thaumaturgist*.

In Swedenborg's grand science of correspondence, to move signifies to live. (*Arcana Celestia*, 5605.) Life is a force, and all force is a form of motion. The movements of the body, both voluntary and involuntary, originate in the soul, and are only modifications of the life of the soul. If your arm is lame, it is because life is retreating from it. Therefore follow the prescription of Jesus, "Stretch forth thine arm." For the motion of the limb will determine an influx of the Universal Life into it. For as motion is life, so immobility is disease and death.

> "Act, act in the living Present!
> Heart within, and God o'erhead.
>
> "Let us, then, be up and doing,
>   With a heart for any fate;
> Still achieving, still pursuing,
>   Learn to labor and to wait."

That state of consciousness which we denominate pain, is not in the material body. Its location there is an illusion and a false belief. Pain, like everything in nature and in the human body, has a mental side to it. It corresponds to something in the mind, which is the cause of it. If we can find this mental or spiritual root of it, from which it arises, and without which it cannot exist, and can remove it, we cure it. To aid us in doing this, we would observe that there are three classes of sensations, which include all our possible sensational experiences.

In the first place is that large class of sensations which may with propriety be denominated indifferent sensations, because our mental attitude toward them is one of indifference. We do not care whether they go or stay. We have neither desire for them nor aversion toward them. They are consequently neither pleasurable nor painful. For this cause they are out of consciousness most of the time. We become conscious of them only by a special act of attention to them. Such is the feeling of the air on the surface of the body when it is neither too warm nor too cold. Such also is the sensation occasioned by the contact of our clothing with the skin. The larger portion of our sensations belongs to this class. Our mental state in relation to them is one of indifference — an equilibrium of desire and aversion which we call contentment.

There is another class of sensations which we denominate pleasurable. The pleasure may exist in a thousand different degrees of intensity, all depending upon our varying mental states in reference to them. Our mental attitude towards this class of sensible experiences is not one of indifference or neutrality, but of desire. We like them and cherish them. It is to be observed that the more of this desire we have, the more intense is the sensation of pleasure; for the pleasure, when we get round to the spiritual side of it, is nothing but that desire; and the pleasure cannot exist without the desire. As a familiar illustration of this general principle in the philosophy of human nature, we know that the more thirsty we are, that is, the more we desire water, the more pleasure we experience in drinking it. Without the thirst in some degree, there is no pleasure in drinking the purest water on earth. The more hungry a man is, that is, the more intense his desire for food, the better his food tastes to him. Without appetite, which is only a name for desire, the richest viands afford no pleasure in the eating. Desire is the ground of all pleasurable sensations. This is the reason why the same thing may be pleasurable to one person, and painful or unpleasant to another. It is owing to the difference in the feelings or mental attitude of the two persons toward it. The one *likes* it; the other *dislikes* it, which are only other names for desire and aversion. What is pleasurable to us at one time may be unpleasant or painful to us at another time, from the law of sympathy and antipathy, or desire and aversion.

There is another class of sensations, which we designate pain. The pain may exist in a thousand degrees of vividness or intensity. The too great sourness of an orange or an apple is pain. Anything we *dislike* is painful to us, and in exact proportion to the degree in which we dislike it. Our mental attitude towards this class of sensations is not one of indifference, as in the first class, nor of desire, as in the second, but of *aversion*, and oftentimes an *impatient haste* to be rid of them. We consider it a fixed principle, as immutable as any law of geometry, *that the more of this aversion and impatience we feel, the more intense is the pain*. The one is the exact measure of the other. The pain on the spiritual side of it is nothing but this feeling of aversion and impatient haste to be delivered from the sensation. If we can bring ourselves to feel that the pain is not an *evil*, but a good, and that all good is desirable and delightful, and remove from our minds the repugnance to it, and replace it by a state of perfect patience and tranquil endurance, the pain will subside and finally cease. Swedenborg defines pain to be a feeling of repugnance arising from *interior falses*, for that which is repugnant to us is painful. (*Apocalypse Revealed*, 697.) In its spiritual essence pain is a feeling of repugnance, and the aversion we feel toward it arises from a misapprehension of its nature and use. It springs from our falsely viewing it as an *evil*, whereas it is always a good. The correction of this deep-seated delusion is the cure of it. All men love and desire what is good, and we cannot avoid this, for it belongs to our nature. And what we love and desire affords us delight, and never pain. If we can remove from our mind the aversion to what we call pain, under the mistaken notion that it is an evil, the pain will go with the aversion out of our consciousness. There is not a law of nature or mind more certain in its operation than this. Pain is caused by our interfering with and obstructing the optimism of nature. The divine life in the world, and in the human body, always works in the direction of our supreme good. And when we can say, not as a prayer for something we have not, but as a state into which we have entered, " Thy kingdom come, and thy will be done in earth (or in the material body) as it is done in heaven," our pain will cease. If the pain we feel, as that of a boil, is a good thing (and it certainly is not an evil or a disease, but an effort of nature towards the renewal of our life), then by viewing it as such, and laying aside our aversion or repugnance to it, and our impatience and the divergence of our will from the Supreme Will, it will change the nature of it, for all good is pleasant to us.

In regard to any painful disease, when we perceive and affirm that what occasions the pain is not an evil, but a good, and when by the light of the supreme knowledge which dispels all our illusions and sensuous fallacies, we view it as a good, our repugnance or aversion to it ceases, and as that is the causal source of the pain, that also disappears from consciousness. For an effect must cease on the removal of its cause. The principles of this chapter will stand the test of experiment. I have known persons in the deepest agony to find immediate and permanent relief by an application of them. Let us remember that our real self, the spirit of man, is included in the Divine Being, and into this great habitation never tear or sorrow came. What we call pain is an illusion. It is a positive good, and all good is delightful. When we view things in the light of the supreme truth, or as the Divine Mind views them, and bring our will into line with the will that creates and governs all, our pains and petty sorrows fall off "like drops of rain from a lotus leaf." An eternal rest, a solid and enduring peace, closes round the soul of him who dwells in God.

The sensual principle, says Swedenborg, is the ultimate of the life of man's mind, adhering and cohering to the five bodily senses. The principle of sense is designed to be entirely subservient and obedient to the intellectual principle. It is influenced and governed by thought and is in fact a mode of thought. There is a *sensus communis*, a common sense, a universal principle of sensation, in which all particular sensation subsists. Thought directed to a part, as in the act of attention, causes a concentration of this principle to the part, and intensifies sensation, and occasions an increased consciousness of pain. To put a sensation of either pleasure or pain out of thought is to remove it wholly from consciousness. The word sense is derived from the Latin *sensus*, which is the passive participle of the verb *sentio*, which means not only to feel, but also to think. Sensation means that which is thought; as idea means what is seen or known. Sensation is a mode of thought, and whether it be a pain or a pleasure depends upon how we think and feel in regard to it. If, as we said before, we think it an evil and consequently feel a repugnance toward it, the sensation will and must be a pain. If we think it a good, and feel no repugnance to it, then it will not be a pain.

CHAPTER X.

THE INFLUENCE OF MIND ON MIND, OR THE DOCTRINE OF MENTAL SPHERES, AND ITS PRACTICAL APPLICATION TO THE CURE OF DISEASE.

The influence which our minds exert over other minds without the use of spoken words, and independent of the ordinary channels of communication through the five senses, is a subject of great importance and constitutes the foundation of a practical system of Phrenopathy or Mental Therapeutics. It has long been known, because it is a matter of frequent experience, that when a person in a melancholy frame of mind comes into a company, though he may not utter a word, he casts a dark shadow over the whole group. His influence would be felt, even though he came in unrecognized. So, on the other hand, if a person in a cheerful and healthful frame of mind comes into a company who are cast down, his unseen, but not unfelt, influence, tends to elevate them to a higher and better mental condition. His atmosphere (or the emanation of his *atma*, or spirit) is beatific, and has the power to bless and make happy all who are within its range of action. This recognized feeling of sympathy of mind with mind plays a very important part both in the generation of diseased conditions and in their cure. We need to study the laws that govern its action, and then it can be made available in the phrenopathic method of cure. We are mysteriously connected with each other. Pythagoras is reported to have said, "that if there is one suffering soul in the universe, all other souls will be affected until that suffering soul is restored to health." This may seem an exaggerated statement, but there is in it a great truth. As is said in a fine little work on psychology recently published: "It is commonly known that two instruments tuned to the same key, and placed sufficiently near each other, are in such harmony that when one is struck, the corresponding key in the other vibrates in unison. We seem to be such instruments." (*Beyond the Sunrise*, p. 85.) The gift of healing seems to be a natural endowment. Persons possessing it will cure by the mental method or any other. Their spiritual atmosphere is charged with a sanative contagion. Their presence and their touch are healthful to the mind and body of a patient. We all know of such physicians. Their very presence is a medicine. The sphere of their mental life is more potent than their drugs. It is the action of mind upon mind. Says Dr. Mayo, Professor of Physiology and Anatomy, in King's College, London: "The mind of a living person in its most normal state, is always, to a certain extent, acting exoneurally, or beyond the limits of the bodily person." This is very far from being a new truth, but its introduction into medical science will be the dawn of a new day. This principle was long ago recognized and promulgated in the system of mental philosophy taught by Swedenborg. He says: "There goes out, yea, flows forth, from every man a spiritual sphere from the affections of his love, which sphere encompasses him, and infuses itself into the natural emanations from the body, so that the two spheres are conjoined; that a natural sphere is continually flowing forth, not only from man, but also from beasts, yea, from trees, fruits, flowers, and also from metals, is a thing generally known; in like manner, in the spiritual world; but the spheres flowing forth from subjects in that world are spiritual, and those which emanate from spirits and angels are thoroughly spiritual, because with them there are affections of love, and thence interior perceptions and thoughts; all of sympathy and antipathy has hence its rise, and likewise all conjunction and disjunction, and according thereto presence and absence in the spiritual world, for what is homogeneous and concordant causes conjunction and presence, and what is heterogeneous and discordant causes disjunction and absence." (*Conjugial Love*, 171. *Dictionary of Correspondence*, under the word *Sphere*.) This emanative mental influence is as much a fact in the realm of mind as is the odorous exhalation of the rose, or the night-blooming cereus. Can it be made available in a system of mental therapeutics?

Few persons ever realize the potential influence of *thought* when directed towards another person, either near or far off in space. On this subject we said, in a work published twenty years ago, which we take the liberty of reproducing here, "It is a fact as well established as any principle of chemistry, that one mind can impress its thoughts and feelings upon another mind without the intervention of spoken words." This fact has been recently established by the Society for Psychical Research in England, an association composed of men eminent in every department of science and literature. In the published reports of the committee on Thought Transference, it has been demonstrated beyond the possibility of doubt, that *ideas* in one mind can be reproduced in another mind, and oftentimes with perfect accuracy. If this is proved, it lays a firm scientific foundation for the system of mental healing. The question to be settled is thus clearly stated by Professor W. F. Barrett: "Is there, or is there not, any existing or attainable evidence that a vivid impression or a distinct idea in one mind can be communicated to another mind without the intervening help of the recognized organs of sensation?" The conclusion arrived at after patient investigation and cautiously conducted experiments, is thus guardedly expressed by him: "I am inclined to believe that other mental phenomena —

such, for instance, as the influence of one mind upon another across space without the intervention of the senses — demand a prior investigation. That cases of such mental action at a distance do really exist I, in common with others, have some reason to believe." To this influence of mind upon mind at a distance, they give the appropriate name of *telepathy*, a combination of two Greek words which express that idea. A quarter of a century ago we instituted a series of experiments, conducted with care, and some of them when the subject was removed from us several hundreds of miles. The conclusion at which we arrived, we stated to be, "that it is a law of our being, from the operation of which we cannot escape, that every time we *think* of an absent person we affect him for good or evil." How careful then should we be to think of the absent kindly, charitably, *prayerfully*, and cheerfully. For if we are sad and despondent, we may cause them to be depressed in spirit, through this telepathic influence ; and if our thoughts of them are expressed in the form of prayer, springing out of a heart overflowing with love and good will, through the law of unconscious sympathy, they may be cheered and strengthened, they know not how. To think of another interiorly and abstractly occasions a spiritual presence of that other ; distance is annihilated, and his living image and inner personality seem to stand before us, and what we say to *it*, we say to him. When the thought is grounded in love and good will, it causes an interior conjunction of minds, a mental sympathy, a condition of *rapport*. By it we come into a living communication as real as it would be if we reached through the intervening space and grasped each other by the hand. The feelings of each are transmitted to the other. The mental state of the one who is the most positive will predominate and take possession of the other, for the stronger force will prevail over the weaker. In this way a morbid mental condition of a patient may be loosened or removed, and a healthier mental state be made to take its place in his consciousness.

The nature and laws of this direct or indirect action of mind upon mind, and the transference of thought and ideas from one mind to another, is a subject of vast practical importance in its relation to the phrenopathic method of cure. It is the cardinal principle on which the whole system of mental healing is based. And it is important that we understand the laws that govern this transmission of thought and the conditions under which it most readily takes place. In the experiments of the Society for Psychical Research, the *modus operandi* was essentially this. A subject was selected who was supposed to be more or less sensitive to thought impulses from other minds. He was blindfolded, in order to shut off from his mind the images of surrounding objects, and left in his normal state without inducing upon him the hypnotic condition. He is seated in a chair with his back towards the agents or operators, with pencil and paper on a stand by his side. A curtain may be drawn across the room so as to render any communication, except by thought, impossible. Then the agent, or agents, as the case may be, draws a figure on paper or cardboard. We will take as an example, a triangle. We look at it with attention; then we close the eyes, and there arises in our minds a mental picture or image of the triangle. This is an *idea*. We now intently *think* of the subject, and in a minute or two he removes the bandage from his eyes, and with the pencil draws the figure on paper, copying it from the *idea* in his mind. Here the mind of the agent comes into such conjunction with that of the subject that the operations of the one are reproduced or reflected in the other. The thoughts, ideas, and even feelings of one mind arise into consciousness in another mind. Sometimes the agent had his hands in contact with the subject, but this was found not essentially to facilitate the tranference of thought. A great variety of figures were drawn on paper, some of them natural objects, and some of them were fantastic. They also experimented with the names of persons and places. And even whole sentences, such as "*Thou shalt not kill*," or "*be kind to animals*." These were reproduced correctly. In impressing a sentence like the above upon the mind of a sensitive, we form in the mind a distinct mental picture or idea of each word and each letter, and then the words arise in the mind of the subject in varying degrees of vividness. All these interesting experiments in thought transference have been collected into a useful little volume by Mr. William A. Hovey, of Boston, entitled *Mind-Reading and Beyond*. But they seem, at first thought, to be trivial and of no value, — mere curious phenomena of mind. Their value as established facts consists in illustrating an important principle. Are there not higher uses of that principle? As the falling of even a pin to the floor illustrates and exhibits the action of the great law of gravitation, so these apparently trifling experiments in thought transference illustrate one of the most important principles in the world of mind, as gravitation does in the realm of matter.

Thought and existence are identical. I exist because I think, and I think because I exist. From this established principle it follows that a change of thought modifies our existence. Ideas, which are thoughts assuming a fixed form, are things; and it has been demonstrated that they are transmissible from one mind to another. Our ideas may excite like ideas in the mind of another, in a way analogous to that in which a sound repeats itself in an echo, or an image of ourself is created in a mirror. In accordance with these established principles, suppose we are called to a person who is suffering from some form of disease, which is the ultimate expression in the body of a wrong way of thinking. Every intelligent physician in his treatment, counts on the natural tendency of the organism towards health. It is the normal condition of all living beings. It is the divine idea of man, and the trend of everything in the world of mind is toward perfection. Suppose we form in our mind the *idea* that the patient *is* recovering, and that he will soon be well, and this becomes in us a *faith*, may not our idea be transferred to him either consciously or unconsciously, and may it not add a new impulse to the life forces in the direction of that result? In this case our idea is not a false one, for our faith is the belief of the truth. No good reason can be given why our idea may not be transferred to his mind, as well as the mental image of the triangle in the case mentioned above, and that idea may accelerate his recovery. Says the learned Professor Bush: "I know that the conceptions of my own mind have been reproduced in another mind without any outward signs, and I know I have not been deceived as to the facts averred." But why may not a physician's better way of thinking, and his sphere of faith and hope, be made to take the place of the morbid mental state of a patient? Our mental states are naturally diffusive and ideas are communicable. An English gentleman, writing in the *Nineteenth Century*, claims to have some six hundred well authenticated cases, where parties separated by many miles of space, were contemporaneously informed of events then taking place. (*The New Philosophy*, by Albert W. Paine, p. 65.) Such a phenomenon is not a miracle, but takes place in perfect harmony with the laws of mind under certain conditions. What are those conditions, and what are those laws?

In the cure of disease by the phrenopathic method, is the action of our mind upon the mind of the patient direct and immediate, or is it effected through an intermediate principle, in analogy with the transmission of the sensation of sound through the Universal Æther? When we telegraph a friendly message from Boston to London, no imponderable fluid shoots along the wire; there is only the transmission of a force, a vibratory wave in an elastic medium which modern science calls the ether. So when one mind acts upon another mind, and influences its thoughts and feelings, when the bodies which they animate may be separated by many miles of space, or may be in the same room, the effect is produced in a similar way. There is only the transmission of a mental energy, and the action and reaction of one mind or spirit upon another. And this takes place in an all-pervading, all-surrounding, and everywhere present principle a thousand times more subtle and vital than anything known to science. We may denominate it with the Hindus, the Akasa; with the Rosicrucians, the astral light; or with the Platonists, the *anima mundi*, or world-soul; or we may adopt the name given to it by Jesus, and call it the Holy Spirit: it is essentially the same thing under various designations. A humble disciple of Jesus need not feel it to be presumption to ask and to expect the aid of that emanative divine principle of life and light, which is called the Holy Spirit, to aid his curative mental effort, and act the part of the "heavenly dove," to bear the quickening influence to the diseased and unhappy patient. It is the function of the Holy Spirit, as we are taught by Jesus, "to convince the world of sin (or of the errors of their understanding) and of righteousness (in the Platonic and esoteric sense of spiritual truth, or of truths that lie above and beyond the range of the senses) and of judgment to come (or to effect a separation of the error from the truth in our minds)." Now these are exactly the things to be done in curing disease by the phrenopathic method. "The Holy Spirit convinces the world of sin," says the Christ, "because they believe not in me (the personification of spiritual truth); and of righteousness, because I go unto my Father (the infinite fountain of all spiritual life and light); and of judgment, because the prince of this world is judged (or the dominating false opinions of the age in which we live, and which are a strong current that bear men onward to disease and death, are put down as a ruling power)." (John xvi: 8-11.) And through Jesus and the Holy Spirit, which he sends in his *name*, or in the quality of his own life, men may come into receptive communication with the great currents of truth and life, which forever flow from God and heaven into the world of angels and men on the earth.

It was found by the investigations of the Committee on Thought Transference, of the Society for Psychical Research, that "strength of will" has no particular effect, except so far as both subject and agent may exercise it in patient attention. What we need is to be able to form in our own minds a clear and distinct conception of the words or ideas which we desire to impress upon the mind of the subject. So in the cure of disease by this method, one would quite naturally suppose that an intense mental effort, or what is usually called will, would be necessary to any favorable result. But this is a mistake, as has been proven by the experiences of many years. It is our business only to *think* the truth (and under the proper conditions to *affirm* it verbally), and then to leave the truth to have everything its own way. An effort of will adds nothing to its force. The more we lose sight of self, in our curative effort, and the more we trust in God, in the Christ, and in the Holy Spirit, the better it will be for us and for the patient. When a person is in a state of passivity or mental inertia, his mind is a *carte blanche*, or white paper, ready to be inscribed with the truth. If a patient is actuated by a sincere *desire* of recovery, and is predisposed to believe you, and trusts in you, and has no repugnance or antipathy to you, it constitutes an affinitive attraction for your higher thoughts and feelings. His mind is open to the impact of your mental influence. Your thoughts of truth, your feelings of faith and hope, leave their impress upon the tablet of his mental being for all time to come, like the tracks of the gigantic birds of a former geological age upon the then soft and yielding sandstone rocks of the Connecticut River valley. Mental impressions will endure when inscriptions on marble or granite rock have worn away and become illegible. It should be our aim and wish, not merely to impress *our* thoughts upon a patient's mind, but to lift *him* from a lower to a higher plane of thought. There are two worlds or ranges of existence, — the spiritual world and the natural or psychical world. Both these worlds are included in the mind of man. The natural world, being the lower region of the mind, is the seat of disease; the spiritual world, being the uppermost region of the mind, is the region of health and true blessedness. To elevate a patient from the plane of sense, "the horrible pit and miry clay," into the spiritual realm of his being, is to place him beyond the reach of all possible maladies. The natural world, including the human body, is not the *real* world. It is in itself vanity, or emptiness. It is *maia*, or illusion. Matter, as a deceptive appearance, is the prison of the immortal spirit, the real man and son of God. To terminate this unnatural bondage, and convince the patient of the unreality of the body and its diseases, is to cure him. If we can do no more, we can *think* this eternal truth for him, and the sphere of our minds may influence him. We may pass into the spiritual realm of thought ourselves, and then, as Jesus does, being lifted up, we draw men unto us. As the poet Wordsworth expresses it: —

> " We are laid asleep
> In body, and become a living soul;
> While with an eye made quiet by the power
> Of harmony, and the deep power of joy,
> We see into the life of things."

The Committee on Thought Transference come to the conclusion, as they state in their report, that the "psychical telergy," or the "telepathic impact," or, to translate it into ordinary language, the influence of our ideas and mental suggestions, falls upon the sub-conscious region of the mind of the subject, and then emerges into consciousness by whatever channel happens in each case to be the easiest. (*Report for July*, 1884, p. 121.) In giving the mental treatment for disease, the patient at the time may not be conscious of any effect produced, and yet in time, perhaps the next day, he becomes sensible of improvement. Because a person feels no influence, like that of electricity, is no proof that he is not benefited by the treatment. Mental and spiritual impressions made on the unconscious or preconscious region of the mind, or on the *substance* of the mind, may be like the picture on the negative plate of the photographic artist, invisible at first, but nevertheless really there, and which by the action of certain chemical agents is made to appear for all time to come. In the transference of ideas from our mind to that of another, the picture is imperceptible at first, but gradually emerges into consciousness. There are some persons who are extremely sensitive to the action of other minds, but they are not always more readily cured by the phrenopathic method than others who are less impressible. The case of a young female, by the name of Euphrosine is mentioned by M. Barrier, a physician of Privas, in a communication to Dr. Foissac, published forty years ago, who possessed so perfectly the gift of divining the thoughts of the person with whom she happened to be, that she readily kept up a very well-connected conversation, in which one of the interlocutors spoke only *mentally*. (*Mesmer and Swedenborg*, by Professor George Bush, p. 43.) Many cases of this kind have existed and been recorded. But such extreme sensitiveness is very far from being necessary in patients who subject themselves to the phrenopathic method of cure.

In the experiments of the Society for Psychical Research, the subjects were in their perfectly normal condition. But they state that they have a large amount of evidence which conclusively shows that transference of thought (and even sensation and feeling) occurs far more readily when the percipient is under the magnetic influence, or is in the *hypnotic* state. (*Report for July*, 1883, p. 173.) This is what has been known for many years. The magnetic sleep is not necessary or even desirable, but only enough of the magnetic influence, to render the patient impressible to your thought-impulses, to induce upon him a state of passivity and *rapport*, and to incline him to accept and believe the *truth* you affirm and suggest, either verbally or mentally. Magnetism is only the influence of one mind on another mind, and through the mind on the body. Says the learned Professor Bush: "The main phenomena of magnetism are *mental*. They involve the laws of *mental communication* between one spirit and another." Again he says: "The transfer of thought may perhaps be regarded as the cardinal fact of the magnetic developments. In the whole category of its marvels there is nothing more wonderful — nothing more difficult to believe, yet nothing more easy to prove." (*Mesmer and Swedenborg* (1847), pp. 15, 53.) In this higher and true meaning of the word magnetism, there can be no reasonable objection to applying it to the mental-cure system. It is only magnetism in its higher spiritual applications and uses. But there is no occasion for controversy about names. A rose would smell as sweet under any other name, yet the old name is like an old and tried friend with whom we do not like to part. In the mental system of cure, as in the phenomena of magnetism, ideas and saving truths are transferred from one mind to another, and what is subjective in our mind becomes an objective reality to the patient, for *ideas* are causes. In a review of the *Primitive Mind-*

Cure, the literary editor of the New York *Tribune* very truly remarks: "It is a part of the mysterious processes of mind, that subjective ideas may become as real, nay, even more real, than objective phenomena; and this is one of the clews to Mind-Cure." This is all that we claim for the system. Our higher and better *idea* of man and of the patient, when transferred to his unconscious mind, may be developed into consciousness and actuality as a vital impulse in the direction of its full realization in the physical organism. It may stimulate and accelerate the natural reaction of the vital powers against disease, and increase the tendency to health and happiness. In sickness the sphere of a sympathetic friend is the best of all medicines for the soul or the body. As a messenger sent from God, he comes to the help of the Lord (one of the designations of the universal saving and healing principle), against the mighty. The system of drug medication has had, and still has, its uses. But is there not a higher and more efficient method of cure? Does drug medication belong to Christianity? Did Jesus and the apostles deal in pills and potions? And did they not cure even organic diseases? While not discarding a true medical science, may we not learn more at the feet of Jesus? Laying aside, forever, the diabolical cruelties of vivisection, which ought to make a savage hide his face for shame, let us study the inner nature of man, and the undeveloped powers and potentialities of mind. Happily for the world, advanced minds in the medical profession are beginning to feel that man is something more than his anatomical structure, and that there are other and better remedies than poisonous drugs. And this feeble light of the dawn, which is hardly distinguishable from the darkness, will grow into a new day.

The system of mental healing, which is exciting so much interest in every part of the country, is no new thing in the world either in its philosophy or practice. It is only the reappearance under the mask of another name of one of the fundamental principles of Christianity, *the doctrine of salvation by faith*, using the word faith in its primitive Christian and Platonic sense of a higher form of knowledge. It is the cognition of spiritual realities and verities which are beyond the ken of the psychical mind of man. The cure of disease by this modern phrenopathic method is only the old primitive doctrine of *conversion*, by which is signified a complete inversion of a person's way of thinking, the turning about of the subject of it from the life of sense to the dominion of the spirit. If it is not this, it is of no great value. The term conversion seems to have been used by Jesus to designate the mental side of the change which took place in healing the diseased. He says of the sensuous Jews of his day: "This people's heart is waxed gross, and their ears are dull of hearing, and their eyes they have closed; lest haply they should perceive with their eyes, and hear with their ears, and understand with their heart, and be converted (or turn about), and I should heal them." (Matt. xiii: 15. Mark iv: 12.) The cures effected by Jesus were a radical change in the mental *status* of the patient, and no half-way affairs. The body was saved from disease by redeeming the soul from the dominion of sin, or the illusion of the senses, and the life of iniquity to which it led. This was the system of spiritual cure eighteen centuries ago, and it is returning to the world to-day. But the Christ, as the personification of the principle of spiritual enlightenment, has so long been absent from the various warring systems called Christianity, through the prevalence of materialism, or what Hegel forcibly denominates the "dirt philosophy," that when he comes again to his old home in the church and the world, it has seemed proper to introduce him to the modern members of the ecclesiastical family under another name, as the old names had become empty of meaning. But as Christianity comes to have a deeper meaning in the minds of men, the old names, as the appropriate vessels for the containing and expressing the truths of the kingdom of God, will come back into use, and the ancient wine of spiritual truth will again fill out the old empty bottles. And the new patch that is now being put into the old threadbare Christian garment, will grow into a complete and connected whole; the robe without a seam which Jesus wore, and which in the science of correspondence signifies a harmonious and perfect system of spiritual doctrine. As it was in the days of yore so will it be again, that he who touches but the hem or fringe of it will be made whole. In the present mental cure system, I know of no principle which is true that is not found in the New Testament and in the true spiritual philosophy of all ages and nations. He who carefully studies that development of Christianity which we have in the writings of Swedenborg will find all the truth there is in the various schools of mental cure. And his spiritual philosophy is nothing but a reproduction and amplification of the ancient Hermetic and Kabalistic science. It would be a very difficult, and even impossible, achievement to produce an absolutely new truth in philosophy or religion. The mental history of the race repeats itself in regularly recurring cycles. In the revolving wheel of life the early Christian method of cure by faith, and which through the prevalence of materialism and sensualism had descended to the bottom of the circle, is now coming uppermost again under the name of phrenopathy or mind-cure. But names are arbitrary and changeable, while principles are immutable. A skillful botanist would recognize the pink, the *Dianthus* or flower of God, even though the people where it grew should call it a lily. So in the modern system of mental healing we recognize the operation of that principle in the Hebrew theosophy which was called Raphael, the divine physician, only the redeeming angel comes to us in a modern dress and in the imperfect disguise of another name.

CHAPTER XI.

PHRENOPATHY, OR MENTAL CURE, AS A PRACTICAL SYSTEM.

IN the present chapter it is our purpose to give in a condensed form all that is necessary for one to know in order to the practice of the phrenopathic method of cure in his family and among his friends. The practical application of the philosophical principles, which have been discussed in the preceding pages, to the cure of ourselves and others is extremely simple, and can be learned by any person of ordinary intelligence, in a brief time. We have given in the series of works which we have published during the last twenty years on the subject of Mental Therapeutics, especially in the two volumes which immediately precede this, the fundamental principles in the practice of the system of mental healing. Little more need be said, and in the present state of knowledge on the subject but little more can be said. There is a great deal of babble about things that have no practical value, and have no more relation to an established system of phrenopathy than they have to astronomy or geology. The following principles have been used by the author for nearly a quarter of a century, and may be viewed as established rules in the phrenopathic method of cure.

In accordance with the principles unfolded in the preceding chapter relating to the influence of mind on mind and the doctrine of the silent influence of our mental sphere upon others, it would seem to be a matter of the first importance that we should be ourselves well and happy, for the universal life-giving principle flowing through us will partake of the quality of the medium through which it flows, just as the light of heaven passing through colored glass emerges from it with the particular color of the substance through which it is transmitted. When we are in a sound mental, and consequently physical, condition, a saving influence may be communicated to others through us. When a person has passed out of death into life, he naturally desires to be the means of helping others. (1 John iii : 14.) The words of Jesus to Peter have a special application to all such, " I have prayed for you that your faith fail not : and when thou art converted (or turned from the life of sense to the life of the spirit), strengthen (or establish) thy brethren." (Luke xxii : 32.)

Every perfectly healthy person is a contribution to the general well-being of the collective humanity. The sphere of his life is a valuable acquisition to the race in its organic unity. Every sick, sinful, unhappy, and complaining invalid is, so far as his influence goes, a public calamity, a diseased and sore spot in the body of the universal man. He roils the current of the world's life, and a great many of them make the water of life very muddy.

The phrenopathic and Christian method of cure is essentially a system of instruction. The doctor is the teacher, as the word itself implies. He aims to bring the patient into his own mode of thought and feeling. We can teach by verbal instruction or by the silent sphere of our life. But we cannot impart by any method what we do not possess. What we have not and are not we cannot give. On this subject Emerson has well said : " If a man can communicate himself, he can teach, but not by words. He teaches who gives, and he learns who receives. There is no teaching until the pupil is brought into the same state or principle in which you are ; a transfusion takes place ; he is you, and you are he ; then is a teaching ; and by no unfriendly chance or bad company can he ever quite lose the benefit. But your propositions run out of one ear as they ran into the other." Again, on the subject of the communication of thought by our silent mental sphere, he says: "That which we *are* we shall teach, not voluntarily, but involuntarily. Thoughts come into our minds by avenues which we never left open, and thoughts go out of our minds through avenues which we never voluntarily opened." (*Essays*, First Series, pp. 122, 127.)

When a person is himself in a cheerful and normal state of mind, and consequently in a healthy condition physically, and sitting or standing near an invalid who has no feeling of antipathy to him, the emanative sphere of his life is always salutary. He surrounds the patient with his own healthier atmosphere, and envelops and pervades his gloom and despair with his life of faith and hope. As to the distance from which we sit or stand in order that this transfusion of thought and feeling may take place most readily, it is said in the report of the Society for Psychical Research, that a distance of three or four feet is best. But that is a matter of little moment. If the mental *rapport* is established, which is the most important thing, it may be three feet or three hundred miles. Nearness and distance in the realm of spirit are not estimated in feet, in miles and leagues, but are *states of the interiors*. We may have a feeling of great nearness and a consciousness of presence of an absent friend, and of utter remoteness from a stranger at our side. In this experience the soul of man begins to assert its freedom from the limitations of space, and gets a fore-gleam of the life eternal.

That manifestation (or emanation) of God which is called Yava (and rendered in our common version of the Scriptures, Jehovah) is the supreme saving and healing principle and power, and is represented by the name of Jesus. As a manifestation of God he is everywhere present, not because he is infinitely *extended* in space, but because he is wholly free from the finite limitations of both time and space. This principle viewed as a person is signified by the Lord, when that word occurs in small capitals in our common version. It is he who forgiveth all our iniquities (or removes from us all the errors of our understanding), and thus healeth all our diseases, and redeemeth our life from destruction. (Ps. ciii: 1–5.) There is no more efficient method of healing ourselves or others than to assume towards this saving power an attitude of peaceful trust, and *let* him save us. They who thus wait upon the Lord, shall renew their strength, or recover back their former vigor of mind and body. (Isa. xl: 31.) Again, it is said by the poet king of Israel, "Blessed (or happy, and consequently healthy) is the man who trusteth in thee," for this angel or emanative principle and messenger of the Lord encampeth round about them that fear him and delivereth them. (Ps. xxxiv: 7, 8.) In our efforts to cure others we can do nothing better than to employ the method of silent trust described in a former chapter. We come into a state of unity with that in which we trust, and likeness to it, and this by a profound law of our being. In the case of idols that are the objects of religious adoration it is said, "They that make them are like unto them, so is every one who trusteth in them." (Ps. cxv: 8, 9.) In the employment of the method of trust, and a silent aspiration of the soul to the Highest and the Best, the mental system of healing and the cure of disease by prayer and faith become one. The cure of mental and physical disease by prayer is based on the recognition of a truth (with often only an obscure and dreamy perception of it), which is expressed by Swedenborg, "that man is so made that he can apply to himself life from the Lord." (*Arcana Celestia*, 4525.) There is a divinely vital and life-giving principle and saving energy, universally diffused, and consequently ever accessible and always available, which is in a perpetual effort to heal us of all our maladies of soul and body. Its existence and ceaseless operation lies beyond the apprehension of sense, and must consequently be perceived and appropriated by *faith*, and grasped by the mind and taken up into our individual being and consciousness by *real prayer*, which is not the repetition of a form of words, but a certain receptive state and attitude of the mind and heart of man. This universal saving energy has the quality and attribute of the Divine Love, that it seeks to impart itself and its immortal blessedness to everything; and the condition of receiving it is to be willing to receive it, to desire it, to hold the soul passively open and upward toward it, and to believe and trust that it *is* saving us. Fichte has truly said, "that we must already be in a certain sense that which we would become in order to become so." (*Destination of Man*, p. 22.) Desire of more and better life is the commencement of it. Hence Jesus affirms, "Ask, and ye shall receive; seek, and ye shall find; knock, and it shall be opened unto you. For every one that asketh, receiveth." (Matt. vii: 7.) This is absolutely true. The reason, the cause, the hidden spring of our asking for more life, or for any spiritual good, is because we have it in a degree already. We must recognize the truth and reality of this. And since belief or faith (which are the same word in the original language of the New Testament) is the ground of all reality, as everything is real to us in the same proportion as we believe it, we come into actual possession and a mental appropriation of it by faith only. God can give us nothing except through faith. Hence Jesus says: "What things soever ye desire, when ye pray, *believe* that ye receive, and ye shall *have*." (Mark xi: 24.) The faith is the reality of the thing itself, for faith is the substance of things hoped for, the evidence of things not seen. (Heb. xi: 1.) Hence it is not only philosophically reasonable, but absolutely certain from one of the deepest laws of our being that the prayer of *faith* will save the sick. And this is no departure from the laws of our nature; in other words, no miracle, but only the operation of a higher law, for in the realm of spirit, what is viewed as supernatural by the psychical mind or man, becomes there the perfectly natural. But in the spiritual state of man prayer lays aside the noisy volubility of the Pharisees, and resolves itself into a tranquil and silent life of trust. It is like the child deeply conscious of his need, who approaches you in silence, casts upon you an imploring look, and holds out his hand to receive what your wisdom and goodness are disposed to give. Neither the ear or hand of God is ever closed against such an appeal.

The attitude of tranquil and silent trust in the Christ, as he who can save to the uttermost, has all the influence attributed by physiologists to "expectant attention," about which they speak. The *idea* of the state to be induced and the change to be effected, is formed in the mind, and in the silence of passive trust we wait its full realization in us. The lesson taught in the passage, of the ancient wisdom, "Be still, and know that I am God," is one of the hardest a nervous invalid has to learn. Silence is the thing to which he is least inclined. But he must be instructed not to *speak* of his troubles; for every time he gives an ultimate expression to them in words, they grow larger in his imagination, and take deeper root. What we most need is rest to our souls, and this we can never have until we cease from our own works. (Heb. iv: 10.) We must lay aside the toiling oar, and float in the current of the infinite Life. As an infant, tired out and exhausted by its fruitless cries, sinks to rest in the maternal arms, so we must cease from our struggles, and sink to rest in the bosom of the manifested God.

> "Wisdom ripens into silence as she grows more truly wise,
> And she wears a mellow sadness in her heart and in her eyes:
> Wisdom ripens into silence, and the lesson she doth teach
> Is that life is more than language, and that thought is more than speech."

In treating a patient by the method of simple trust, we should wait in the silence that lies at the heart of things for the "soundless word" that shall arise out of the eternal Life. In the stillness of our own soul and will, we are to let it speak in us, and through us, to the soul of the patient. There is a divine saving power in it. It is that inward voice referred to by the centurion when he said to Jesus, "Speak the word only, and my servant (or child) shall be healed." An eloquent silence is more effectual than the noisy babble of superficial minds, especially if it is the speaking silence of tranquil trust. Such an unshaken trust is like an immovable rock beaten by a thousand waves of the sea, and turns them all back into the abyss. "Trust ye in the Lord forever: for in the Lord Jehovah (Jah, Java) is everlasting strength," or, literally rendered, a rock of ages. (Isa. xxvi: 4.)

While we are to educate a patient to maintain an obstinate silence in regard to his disease and its symptoms, we are to draw out from him a verbal acknowledgment of his cure, or of any improvement in his condition. He is to avoid anything that might seem a presumptuous boasting, for that often indicates an approaching relapse, but make a humble confession. This confirms and ultimates the belief or faith of a cure, "Because if thou shalt confess the word with thy mouth that Jesus (who represents and personifies the supreme saving principle) is Lord, and shalt believe in thy heart that God hath raised him from the dead (in thee), thou shalt be saved (or healed); for with the heart man believeth unto righteousness (in the Kabalistic and Platonic sense), and with the mouth confession is made unto salvation." (Rom. x: 9, 10.) To give expression to our feelings in words intensifies them and makes them permanent.

We are to educate a patient to look upon what he calls his disease, not as an evil, not as a *disease*, but an effort of the divine life of nature to rid us of the real malady, which is mental, and lies back of all the symptoms. He is not to judge of his so-called malady from the deceptive appearances of the senses, but to look at it from a higher range of the intellect. This may seem a difficult lesson to learn, but it is by no means an impossible one. As is well said by Dr. Jennings, "Accustom yourself to all your little pains and aches, and also in your grave and more distressing affections, to regard the movement concerned in them in a friendly aspect, designed for and tending to the removal of a difficulty of whose existence you were before unaware, and which, if suffered to remain and accumulate, might prove the destruction of the house you live in; and that instead of needing to be cured, it is itself a curative operation, and that which should be called a disease lies back of the symptoms, which, in fact, are made for the express purpose of removing the real disorder or difficulty." These are words of wisdom. By viewing what we call disease in this aspect, and laying aside our feeling of repugnance to it as an evil, we essentially change the nature of it, and remove all obstruction to the divine curative process.

The sentiment of fear, in its Protean forms, plays a most important part in the inception and progress of diseased conditions. It is a fountain that sends forth nothing but bitter waters. Hence it would seem to be the first business of a phrenopathic physician to allay the fears of a patient, which is often equivalent to a cure. Fear is often the keystone of the arch, on the removal of which the morbid structure which the imagination has reared falls to the ground. In many cases an abnormal fearfulness is the mental and real malady. By the law of thought-transference, write upon the unconscious region of the mind of the patient the prescription of Jesus, "Be not afraid; only believe," and, "Peace, be still." Let the calm, tranquil sphere of your own mind be like oil on the troubled waves, and, as in the storm on the lake of Galilee, "the giant waves will sink like sobbing infants to their rest." Before we can work such transformations in the mental condition of a patient, we must be free from fear ourselves, for there is no mental state which is more contagious. "There is no fear in love, but perfect love casteth out fear. He who feareth is not made perfect in love." (1 John iv: 18.) It was the sublime calmness and self-possession of Jesus the Christ which gave him such power over the troubled minds of men.

"Majestic sweetness sat enthroned
Upon the Savior's brow."

On the influence of fear in causing disease, and consequently upon the importance of removing it, an intelligent physician of Davenport, Iowa, writes to *Mind in Nature*, published in Chicago, "that in 1832, before the cholera had made its appearance in the United States, his brother was living in Oxford, Ohio, and when he heard the first news of its probably reaching this country, he became *greatly excited*. He was *sure* he would fall a victim to the disease, he said. His fear increased as further reports came, and before the malady reached New York, he was taken sick with Asiatic cholera, attended with all the concomitant symptoms, and died within twenty-four hours after being attacked." — *Mind in Nature*, May, 1885. It might be proper to ask, Was it really cholera that caused his death? Was it not fear of which he died? The cholera was not the primary, but a secondary disease. The cholera was only a symptom of the real malady.

We have seen in the preceding chapter that the cure of disease by the phrenopathic method is, or should be, the same as that change of *mental status* which in the New Testament is called conversion. The Greek term $\epsilon\pi\iota\sigma\tau\rho\o\phi\eta$ signifies a full and complete turning, as the preposition in the compound word gives intensity of meaning to it. It is a turning, not of the body, but of the mind, from the life of sense to a spiritual mode of thought and feeling. When the psychical or natural man becomes the spiritual man, which transition from the lower to the higher degree of our being is called conversion, the change is described by Jesus as a passing from death unto life. "Verily, verily" (which in the original is *amen*, from the Hebrew *amuna*, truth), "I say unto you, he that heareth my words, and believeth him that sent me, hath eternal life (as a present attainment) and shall not come into condemnation, but hath passed out of death into life." (John v: 24.) So great a change as this ought surely to be nothing less than a transition from disease into health, both of mind and body. It is, in the New Testament sense of the word, a resurrection, for the *anastasis* of which Jesus speaks is not the resuscitation of a dead body in a graveyard, but an ascent in the scale of life from the psychical to the spiritual degree of existence.

In the primitive Christian system, sin and disease are the same. Sin is the mental, and disease the physical, side of the same thing. To cure disease and *forgive* sin, in the fulness of meaning given to that expression by Jesus, are identical. We do not of course use the terms forgiveness of sin in the superficial sense given to them in the popular theology, the mere saving of the guilty from deserved punishment, but in the signification of the original words. The term employed to express the idea of forgiveness ($ἀφίημι$) means to put away or remove a thing. This is in fact the radical meaning of the English word *forgive*. The first syllable, *for*, is the same as the Saxon *far*, and to forgive sins is to put them far away, and you cannot place a thing further away from another than to remove it from thought and from belief. The Latin-English word *remit* has the same meaning, and also the French *pardonner*, where the syllable *par* is the equivalent of the Saxon *far*, and the meaning is to put a thing far away, as, for instance, an error, a sin. This is the forgiveness or pardon of sin that has some saving or healing value in it to the sinner. It is not putting a veil over the sin, but a taking it out of the man's life. The Buddhist doctrine of *Karma* admits of no escape from the results of wrong doing. What a man sows he must of necessity reap. This is in a certain sense true. But a man may stop sowing error and evil, and then he has no more reaping to do of that kind of crop, and both the seed and the harvest may be destroyed. Christianity has revealed to the world the doctrine of the *remission* of sin. Sin may be put away. Our transgressions may be blotted out, that is, expunged from the record of the universal life-principle. It is said of Jehovah, who is represented in the Gospels by Jesus, the supreme saving principle, that he will turn again and have compassion upon us, and subdue our iniquities, and cast all our sins into the depths of the sea. (Micah vii : 19.) That means that they shall be covered from sight, and obliterated from the book of remembrance, which is the universal life. The ocean is very deep, and a thing on the bottom of it is for us practically out of existence. Captain James Ross in the region west of St. Helena sounded to the depth of more than five miles and a quarter, and found no bottom. Our sin (or error) which has led to disease may be put away from us, and covered in the depths of the sea, where it can never be the seed of a future harvest, and we may be placed back on the same footing that we should be if we had never sinned (or erred). This is at least the teaching of Jesus and Christianity. He who practises the phrenopathic method of cure will have occasion to say in the language of the Apostles, "Repent ye therefore, and turn about, that your sins may be blotted out, that so there may come seasons of refreshing from the presence of the Lord, and that he may send the Christ who hath been appointed for you, even

Jesus" (the saving, healing principle and power). (Acts iii : 19, 20.)

In treating a patient by the mental method, it is incumbent on us to ascertain what the underlying sin (or error, false belief) is, and aim to correct it and put it away from him, for it sustains a causal relation to his malady. *It will always be found to be some illusion of the sensuous mind.* We can learn what it is from the statement of the case by the patient, who is generally only too willing to give it. On the development of the intuition in us, we can detect the mental side of a given disease at once, and with well-nigh unerring certainty. And we are to treat that, and not the physical effect. The great mass of mankind are under the powerful dominion of phantasy. An illusive conception may lead, and usually does lead, to an error in the life. Any transgression of the laws of life, any deviation from the divine order of our earthly existence, grieves the Holy Spirit (to use a New Testament expression), which is the divine life-principle, and is that whereby we are sealed unto the day of redemption, or the deliverance from the dominion of the body, and the unnatural lordship of the senses. All such errors of belief, and consequent evils in practice, must be *repented* of, using the term in a philosophic sense. That state of the mind which is denominated repentance prepares the way for the exercise of faith, or that higher form of thought and knowledge by which we are made whole. The original word for repentance ($\mu\epsilon\tau\alpha\nu o\acute{\iota}\alpha$) signifies a change of mind or thought, a change of will or purpose, and is so defined in the standard lexicons. It is not merely sorrow for sin, for a godly sorrow worketh repentance. (2 Cor. vii : 10.) It is not a reformation of the life, for that is the fruit or effect of it, and not the thing itself. When a man is convinced of his error, and rejects it as an evil which is contrary to the divine Will, which is the same as the Infinite Goodness, and thus changes his mind or way of thinking in regard to it, and purposes to think and live differently, he has repented and come into an attitude of mind toward the hurtful error and evil that renders the remission, or putting away, of the sin from him possible. It was a tenet of the Platonic philosophy, that no one ever desires or chooses evil *as* evil, but only under the mistaken conception of it as a good. According to the laws of the mind, evil viewed as such cannot be an object of desire. All deviation from right living is the result of an error of the understanding, — a sin, — and this must be corrected. It is to be also remarked, that to correct an error in ourselves is to come into the opposite truth. If it be an error, an illusion, that I, the immortal Ego and real self, am sick, if the error be removed, I must believe the opposite, that I am well. If my malady is not in my real self, it must be an unreal thing, a delusive appearance. To put away an evil is from a necessary and immutable law to come into the opposite good. If a man ceases to be idle, he must be industrious; if he ceases to be intemperate, he comes into the virtue of temperance. The end of the night is the beginning of the morning. It is our business to correct the error and the evil in a patient; the opposite good and truth will take care of themselves. Here we have a practical application of the highest law of thought, the law of contradictions. Says Sir William Hamilton: "The highest of all logical laws, in other words, the supreme law of thought, is what is called the principle of contradiction. It is this: a thing cannot be and not be at the same time. *Alpha est, Alpha non est* (Alpha is, Alpha is not) are propositions which cannot both be true at once. There is no middle ground that is tenable, and on the principle of excluded middle between two contradictories, while both cannot be true, one *must* be true." (*Lectures on Metaphysics*, p. 526.)

As sickness and health are opposite and contradictory states, and cannot both be predicated of a man at the same time, if we can cause him to perceive and feel that he is not sick, he must feel that he is well, for one must be true. We have all read many times the story of certain medical students making a man in health sick by causing him to *think* and *believe* that he was sick. In the phrenopathic method of cure we simply reverse this process, and make the man well by inducing him to think himself well; not that we would deny the *fact* of the disease, as a state of his consciousness, but simply that the immortal Ego, the spiritual entity and real man, is neither diseased nor unhappy. The disease is in a region of our existence that is below or, what means the same, is external to the *man*, the essentially human nature and principle. How we may best effect this radical change in an invalid's way of thinking of himself is a question of supreme moment, and one which we are called upon to answer.

It is to be done by the simple power of thought, uttered in appropriate words, or symbolic signs, or unexpressed. There is a living force and saving energy in thought. It is thought which shapes and governs the worlds, and it is our thoughts which mould our fate, for thought and existence are one.

> "I hold it true that thoughts are things
> Endowed with being, breath, and wings:
> And that we send them forth to fill
> The world with good results, or ill."

In treating a patient by the mental method, with a kindly positive and affirmative attitude of mind, we are steadfastly to think the *truth* in regard to his inner self, and maintain in our minds the correct *idea* of ourselves and of him; and the silent sphere of our minds, according to the law of thought-transference, will influence him in a degree proportioned to his susceptibility.

The reader would do well to review the subject of the nature and influence of ideas, as given in the first, the eighth, and fifteenth chapters of the preceding volume of the author. The types, patterns, and formative causes of things are called ideas. Ideas have been defined by Hermes Trismegistus as "the forms of the Invisible." God's ideas of things are the causes of the existence of all the objects of nature. Our perfect ideal of the patient transferred to the sub-conscious region of his mind will operate as a cause. After we have thoroughly mastered the doctrine of the triune nature of man, and have learned that the spirit is a personal limitation of the Supreme Spirit, it ought not to be a difficult thing to form the true idea of a patient. Our real life lies deeper than the ken of the psychical man can penetrate; it is more divine than it ever appears to sense. It is hid with Christ in God. Disease and every form of evil are but the driftwood on the surface of the current; deeper down towards the divine centre of all things, our personality, without ever being lost, is forever allied to the infinitude of God. We look away from the surface of a patient's being, become blind to the disease which has its seat only there, and recognize his unchanging, undying, spiritual self alone, which is included in the Christ and is one with the manifested God. We look beyond the *appearance* of life, to its divine reality; for, as Henry James has said, "God is the all of man's life; the power of man is at the bottom the power of God." Hence man — that is, the essentially human principle — is never sick or infirm. There is a saving power in this eternal truth. In disease it is the horn of the altar before which we have taken refuge, and to which we cling with a tenacity of faith whose grasp no earthly power can unloose. We hold to it in spite of the senses and even reason.

Without puzzling ourselves or the patient with speculations as to the origin of evil, we are to recognize the immutable and necessary truth, that God wills to have all men to be saved, and to come to the knowledge of the truth. (1 Tim. ii: 4.) And if we ask anything according to his will, we *know* that he hears us. (1 John v: 14.) The will of God is the Eternal Goodness, and what God wills, *is*. It is said, in a very ancient work of Hermes Trismegistus on Initiations, "that the will of God is absolute accomplishment; to will and to do are for him the work of the selfsame instant." Again: "He who is the fulness of all things, and who possesses all that he wills, wills nothing by caprice. But everything he wills is good, and he has all that he wills. Such is God, and the world is the image of his righteousness." With the manifested God, who is the Christ, the will and the existence of the thing willed are an inseparable unity. Hence, in the Christ, and in the Christ region of our own being, every man is already saved. By faith we view ourselves (and others) as having a salvation in him. We are complete in him who is the head of all principality and power. (Col. ii: 10.) By maintaining this idea of ourselves and the patient, with an obstinacy that is the result of an inward conviction, this subjective salvation which we have in the Christ becomes objective. The ideal, which is the inmost real, will become the actual. As certainly as a seed with its living germ has in it a conatus or tendency to unfold into the perfected plant, so surely does an idea in the mind tend to translate itself into a bodily expression.

If it be a truth that our immortal self is included in the being of the Christ, the universal spirit, and the manifested God, and is already saved and was never lost or diseased, why is it that we are ever sick? It is simply because we are blind to that truth of faith, in consequence of the soul's immersion in the life of sense. It is hidden from the perception of the psychical man. The earth turns on its axis once a day; yet, if our judgment were governed wholly by our sense-perceptions, it would not be to us a reality, any more than it is to animals. To such a man it is an unknown truth, and it is the same to him as if it were not. So until the supreme truth that our inmost being and real self is in the Christ, and the Christ in us is the real self, is apprehended by thought, and we attain to a certitude of belief of it, it is not to us a conscious reality. An unrecognized truth has no influence over us. We are saved by the *knowledge* of the truth. Millions of people are born and pass through their earthly existence, eat, drink, toil, sleep, and die, with no thought of their celestial and undying self. They think downward, and never once look up. To change all this is the aim of the phrenopathic physician.

To modify a patient's thinking in regard to himself and his disease, we employ the principle of suggestion or positive *affirmation*—not mental argument, as it is sometimes called, for argument creates doubt and reaction. No sick man was ever cured by reasoning with him, mentally or verbally. It is the business of the man who *knows* the truth, not to argue, but to *affirm*. The spiritual man judgeth all things, but is himself judged by no one. (1 Cor. ii: 15.) If he is endued with power from on high, he will possess the ability to fasten saving, healing impressions upon the minds of men. The influence of suggestion and positive affirmation upon a person in the hypnotic state borders upon the miraculous, and is attracting deserved attention among physiologists in Europe, and has ever since Professor Heidenhain called the attention of scientific men to it. In France, at Nancy, M. Focachon was able by his will, expressed in the form of suggestion, to modify the action of the vital organs of his subject, and actually caused a blister to form on her back. But the effect of suggestion is the result of the *faith* of the subject, for it is always proportioned to the degree in which the patient *believes* what you say. If the patient is predisposed to believe you, the magnetic state is not necessary to the influence of your affirmations upon him. If he is not thus disposed, we employ *silent or mental suggestion*, and oftentimes with marvellous effect.

In accordance with the law of thought-transference, and acting on the principle that ideas operate as causes, we form in our minds the idea of the change to be effected in the patient in order to the cure of his disease. We have only space for a few illustrations. In dropsy there is a suspended or defective action of the kidneys and sometimes of the skin. A cure cannot be effected by any therapeutic agent without a restoration of the kidneys to their normal functional action. In rheumatism there is also a defective action of the renal functions. Certain acids, as the lactic, the uric, and lithic acids, are retained in the blood instead of being eliminated from it by the kidneys. In some cases of disease an increased or diminished action of the perspiratory glands of the skin is indicated as necessary, or an increased activity of some one or all of the excreting organs. Whatever the physiological change is which is demanded, the universal life-principle, which we call nature, is making an effort to effect it, and we may augment her curative endeavor by forming in our minds the idea of the change. Here knowledge is power, and we find medical science an auxiliary to the mental system of cure. And we would take occasion to remark, that no *intelligent* practitioner of the mind-cure will ignore wholly all medical science. Mind is the only active principle in the universe. The mind of a skillful surgeon performs marvels in saving the lives of people.

The phrenopathic system is not necessarily antagonistic to other methods of cure, as the various hygienic regulations, and even the use of the harmless specific remedies. Through various agencies the mind may act on the body. From ultraisms and hobbies of all kinds phrenopathy should be kept clear. If you give a harmless specific medicine, or a bread pill, or employ the dilutions and triturations of homœopathy, the patient forms in his mind the *idea* of a certain change in the action of the subtle life forces, and you do the same, and in many cases there is no rational objection to such a course any more than there is to the food we eat and the water we drink, provided always that the remedy is innoxious. He that is not against us is for us, even though he follow not with us. (Luke ix : 49, 50.) The best way of getting from place to place is to walk, for according to correspondence, to walk signifies to live. But if we cannot walk, other modes of locomotion are not to be discarded, such as coaches, horse-cars, and railroads. If a man cannot walk by faith, let him have a carriage, or at least a cane or a crutch. Until we become spiritual enough to glide through space like the gods of Homer, we shall have occasion to use other and slower means of getting about.

A very essential qualification for the practice of the mental-cure system, is the power of mental abstraction, the ability to fix our thought upon one thing and to banish all other things from the mind. This state of mental concentration was called in the Hindu metaphysics *Ekâgrâta*, that is, one-pointedness. The attainment of that power was considered as an indipensable condition of all philosophical speculation and religious development. In order to attain to this abstraction from external things, and concentration of thought, they repeated the holy syllable *Om*, a contraction of *A. U. M.*, the initials of the Hindu trinity, Aditi, Viradj (the *V* is a *U*), and Maia, answering to the Father, Son, and Holy Spirit in the Christian system. The faculty of mental abstraction, and the ability to concentrate the mind upon one thing, is a natural endowment, but can be cultivated by practice.

In order to a successful practice of the mental-cure system, it is not necessary to deny the personality of God as some have done, and reduce him to an inconceivable sea of being, an ocean of spirit without bottom or shore. This is applying to the Divine Being that which can be predicated only of matter, — the quality or property of extension. Such a God would be to us no God. Personality consists in Love and Wisdom, as there is no abstract impersonal love or understanding. The infinity and immensity of God are not boundless space, but the negation of space — absolute freedom from the limitations of space. So the eternity of God is not endless time, but the denial of time. We are to eliminate from our conception of the Deity all ideas of time and space.

Neither is it necessary to deny the personality and persistent individuality of the human spirit. Personality is not predicable of the body, for, as we have shown, the corporeal organism is not man. The mind, or thinking principle, is the man. The feeling that "I am I" is as immortal as the Deity, for it is the perpetual gift of God, and we cannot divest ourselves of that consciousness without annihilation. "The gift of God is eternal life," and he gives life to man so fully that it must ever seem as his own. Even the Buddhist Nirvana is not the annihilation of self, but the destruction of selfishness. Those who attain to it have no desire of separate possessions, but only of that which belongs to all pure souls alike, — like the atmosphere we breathe. In the Christian heaven, what all possess belongs to each, and the good and truth of each is freely imparted to all. Yet heaven is not a countless number of individuals reduced in a crucible to a molten sea of being. The selfhood is not *lost* in Godhood, but the true self, the undiseased and undying spiritual entity, is *found* included in the Christ, who is the manifested God. To believe this of myself will save me, for it is the highest state and act of faith. To steadfastly believe it of another, who has not consciously climbed up to this summit of spiritual intelligence, will tend to save (or heal) that other. For when we are ourselves lifted up, we may draw all men unto us. The cessation of our distinct (not separate) individuality would be equivalent to our annihilation.

It is not necessary to deny the existence of matter, but only to affirm the sovereignty of mind over it. Matter exists as a mode of consciousness in us, and is as real as that mode of thought. So disease exists as a wrong way of thinking, and to change that way of thinking for the belief of the truth, is to cure the disease, of whatever nature it is. It is not necessary to tell a man, dying of consumption, that he is not sick, for that is not true. If he is not sick, why try to cure him? We would only affirm, and if possible, cause him to perceive, that the deepest reality of the disease is not physical, but mental. By a fall on an icy sidewalk a man may break his arm or his leg. We would not cure him by denying the fact of his existence or of the sidewalk, for there is no saving virtue in what is false. But recognizing both the fall and the fracture, we would affirm that the immortal man is not injured, and that no sooner was the wound made than an everywhere-present Divine Life goes to work to heal the hurt. We would steadfastly believe this, and form in our mind the idea of the change to be effected in order to a cure, and aid nature by accelerating the curative process.

As to the use of the hands, we must be guided by our instincts and intuitions when and how to use them. The apostles, by the imposition of the hands, imparted the Holy Spirit, the Universal Life-Principle, and no good reason can be given why it may not be done to-day. As has been well said by my friend, Professor Butts " Jesus often laid hands on the sick and healed them. But it was not the *hand* that healed. It was the moral goodness that was resident in the soul. So far as *hands* were concerned, everybody in Judea had them; but not everybody had the divine wisdom which constitutes spiritual magnetism." (*Hints on Metaphysics*, p. 45.)

In closing the discussion of the subject of Mental Therapeutics in this chapter, we would say in the language of Paul, "There is one God, and one Mediator between God and men, the man Christ Jesus." (1 Tim. ii: 5.) Through Jesus we may have communication with the Father, the Supreme and Eternal Goodness, the τὸ ἀγαθὸν of Plato, the *Summum Bonum*, or highest good. He is the door through which we enter in, the inward Teacher, the way, the truth, and the life. A sympathetic or psychometric conjunction with him places us in a receptive relation to the manifested God and the spiritual realm of being. He came to earth from that region of existence, and in returning left the gates open along the upward and shining way, and heaven has been pouring itself into earth ever since. By connecting ourselves with Jesus, we become "joint heirs" with him of all the Father has to give to men. For he says to the Father, "all mine are thine, and thine are mine." (John xvii: 10.) Through him we come into a fellowship (κοινωνία, conscious community of life, the state of having all things in common) with God, and the blood of Christ, or the light of the Supreme Truth, cleanses us from all sin, — from all false beliefs and the errors of life to which they lead. (1 John i: 7–9.) If there is any higher system of mental cure than this, we have never learned it. It is a way of salvation from sin and disease which will stand the test of experiment. "For we have not followed cunningly devised fables when we made known unto you the power and coming of our Lord Jesus Christ." (2 Peter i: 16.) If we give ourselves to him, he will give us back to God, and we shall receive in return the Divine Life and Supreme Good.

CHAPTER XII.

THE KEYS OF THE KINGDOM OF THE HEAVENS, OR THE POWER TO DELIVER OURSELVES AND OTHERS FROM THE BONDAGE OF THE SENSES.

THAT degree of our mental being which may be characterized as the life of sense, and which is the opposite of the life of the Spirit, is denominated by Paul the *psychical* mind or man, improperly translated in our common version of the New Testament, the natural man. It is the aim of Christianity, as it has ever been of all spiritual religions, to elevate man from this lower plane of thought, which is the seat of all our sin and disease, to the spiritual condition, which is life and peace. In the system of Buddhism, which was once a truly spiritual religion before it became degraded into an external mechanism of rites and ceremonies, the external sense-life is denominated *Mahat* or *Prakriti*. The birth into the spiritual life is called *Moksha* and *Nirvana*, and is that of which Jesus speaks, as entering into the kingdom of the heavens, or the kingdom of God, a condition of spiritual development, or education, that is attainable on earth, and not to be taught, as is usually done, as belonging exclusively to a future state. It is such a state of union with God that the man becomes a part of the grand whole, — the *pleroma* or fulness of being (Eph. iii : 19), — a state where the Divine and Celestial in man come to dominion and reign. But the man is never so absorbed and merged into the Divine Essence as to lose his individuality. Even Nirvana is attainable on earth. The Buddha is represented as teaching that "those who are free from all worldly desires enter Nirvana." (*Precepts of the Dhammapada,* v. 126.) In this state man lives spiritually, and is freed from the bondage of the senses and the controlling influence of their illusions. It is a difficult task to convince an invalid that all his sense-perceptions are a deceptive appearance, and are never to form the basis of his judgment as to his réal condition. But how often do we have to correct the fallacious testimony of our senses. In a winter's day, with the mercury far below the freezing-point, the water of the ocean feels colder to the hand than the air, but it is several degrees warmer. A man in a chill may feel cold when he is five degrees above the normal temperature of the human body. When he is suffering from the heat on a summer's day, if you test him by the thermometer, he may be below the natural temperature of the body. Judging from the testimony of the senses, who would suppose that the earth was a sphere instead of an extended plain? That the planets and fixed stars are worlds, and some of them much larger than the earth? That light, color, and sound are nothing external, but are modifications of mind or states of consciousness which are called sensations. A man on the equator is moving through space, with the revolution of the earth on its axis, at the rate of a thousand miles an hour, yet he has no evidence of it from his senses. He seems to himself to be at rest, which, like all our sense-perceptions, is the opposite of the truth. Real knowledge begins where sensation ends. All genuine science consists in correcting the illusive testimony of our senses. It is the object of mental and spiritual science to raise us out of the dominion of the senses into the light of real truth, or what Kant denominates the pure reason. When a straight stick, as a rosewood cane, is immersed obliquely in water for half its length, it appears to be bent. Our sense of sight testifies to this as positively as it does to anything. But it is not bent;

it is an illusion, a false appearance, an aberration from the truth in the judgment of the psychical man or mind. When we stand on the beach and watch the water of the ocean after a storm, the waves *seem* to rush in upon the land, and ninety-nine persons out of a hundred will affirm this. But they do not. There is only a successive elevation of the water from beneath. If we throw in a stick, it is not washed in upon the land. It only rises up, and is left where it was before.

But we shall be asked, Is it possible for us to correct these deceptive appearances so that they will *appear* to us otherwise, and in accordance with the truth? It is possible and easy. When we *know* that the waves are not rushing in upon the land, they no longer *seem* to do so. To the astronomer the earth does not seem a level plain. He does not form in his mind that conception or idea of it. So a man may come under the fixed influence of the illusion that he is sick; but he is not. The *real* man is not diseased, any more than our rosewood cane is bent by being immersed in water. He has only come to *think* himself sick; but it is a deflection or aberration from the truth. He judges according to the sensuous appearance, which is contrary to the precept of Christianity and to the life of faith. The belief that we are sick is not a "righteous judgment." It is not a divine rectitude of thought, but the judgment is warped. But can a man on a sick-bed make it appear to himself that he is not diseased? We can only answer by saying that it is *possible*. We do not say that it is always an easy matter to do it. We only affirm its possibility. When he has come to the knowledge of the real self, the immortal and undying Ego, the unchanging *I Am*, and views that as his true being, then he *knows* that he is not diseased, and the disease as the creation of a false judgment disappears. A few mornings ago, during a cold wave which swept over

New England, a friend of ours started to walk to the station, a distance of half a mile. The air was perfectly still, the rising sun was shining brightly in an unclouded sky, and the man with no extra protection was not aware of the extreme cold. But he met a neighbor who informed him that the mercury was twenty-four degrees below zero. After this he was nearly frozen before he reached his office. If he had continued in the blissful ignorance with which he started out on his walk, he would have suffered less. The cold is not measured by the thermometer, but is a sensational state in us. We do not wish to be understood as affirming that if all men should agree to *think* and *believe* that it was warm, it would make it so. Such a universal belief would not melt snow and ice, nor affect the mercury in the bulb of the thermometer. *But our belief affects our sensational life.* The man who has never found out that he is sick, is well. Much of what passes current in the world for medical science is well calculated to give to people this hurtful knowledge, and many diseases arise from it. It teaches men how to believe themselves sick, how to find out in the most scientific manner that they have a particular malady. It sets them on the hunt for symptoms of disease, and they are quite sure to find them. But the mental science of health and disease instructs men how to find out that they are not sick, which is the best of all remedies. The poet Churchill, who was an educated physician, gives us a good prescription for most nervous invalids : —

> "The surest road to health, say what they will,
> Is never to suppose we shall be ill;
> Most of the evils we poor mortals know,
> From doctors and imagination flow."

This, though not in the highest strain of poetry, contains some grains of truth, enough for an initial dose in mental medicine. But how can an invalid rise above his illusions?

To be affected by disease is, in the expressive language of the New Testament, to be *bound*. (Luke xiii : 16.) How can we be loosed from our infirmities? How can we straighten our rosewood cane that seems bent in the water? Only by looking at it from a higher plane of the mind. We can break the fetters of illusion only by faith. There is a faith of which Jesus and the apostles speak, which is not a borrowed *opinion*, but a higher knowledge of truth, a state of spiritual perception, an inward divine illumination and intuitive belief, and this celestial knowledge is the power of God and the wisdom of God unto salvation for both soul and body. Through the silent sphere of our life, the unseen influence of our minds, combined with instruction, a patient may be raised to this more elevated plane of thought. In the other life, says Swedenborg, — by which he can only mean the realm of mind, — all thoughts are communicated to those around. (*Heaven and Hell*, 325.) The more deeply we are grounded in the celestial degree of life, the more powerfully will our minds and thoughts affect others. The Christian law of life is well expressed by Paul, "We that are strong ought to bear the infirmities of the weak." (Rom. xv : 1.) The idea in the original is, not merely to bear with, to endure, but to take away, to remove the infirmities of our weak neighbor. The original Greek word is the same as in the passage where it is said of Jesus, " Himself took up our infirmities and bare away our diseases." (Matt. viii : 17.) We are to take away the idea and fallacious belief of disease, and give to the patient, in its stead, the idea of recovery and of health. This we shall be able to do only after we have obtained the keys of the kingdom of heaven, which invests the Christian hierarch with the power of binding and loosing. On a certain occasion, when Jesus was in the region of Cæsarea Philippi, he asked his disciples or scholars, Who do men say that the son of man is? In harmony with the wide-spread and ancient belief in the reincarnation of souls, some thought him to be Elijah, or Jeremiah, or some other of the greater Jewish prophets. The question being put to Peter, he replied, "Thou art the Christ, the Son of the Living God, the *El Chai*, the Mighty Living One." This was revealed to Peter by our Father in the heavens, and not by flesh and blood, or the lower animal soul. It was an inward illumination from the light of the supreme and universal Spirit. And on this truth, as on a rock of ages, that the inmost spirit of man is the son and perpetual offspring of the living God, and that the life of the spirit is the only true and enduring life, and that all other life is an ever-changing and evanescent illusion, the Christ affirms that that state of man which is called the church, and which is heaven on earth and in man, shall be built, and the gates of Hades, or the power and influence of undeveloped souls, the astral realm of being, shall not prevail against it. To such a one the keys of the kingdom of heaven are committed. In the divine science of correspondence a key signifies the power of spiritual truth, a living faith, which can free men's souls from the dominion of Hades, or the fetters of sense. It is the recognition of ourselves and others as sons and daughters of God, and the inward Christ as our true and immortal being. Disease and sin, which belong to Hades, or the astral region in man, the plane of the animal soul and the external senses, cannot invade this divine centre of our existence. Even death itself stops short and turns back on approaching the confines of our true being, unable to approach nearer to its quenchless light of truth. If disease comes forth to attack the outposts of our existence, we may be sure it can never storm the citadel of life in us. From this celestial altitude of our being, the Christ realm of human nature, the summit and crown of life, we may go forth to meet the enemy and turn him back into Hades, and with the key of the house of

David, may lock the door after him; for what we bind on earth shall be bound in the heavens; and what we loose on earth (or set at liberty from sin and disease) shall be loosed in the heavens. (Matt. xvi: 13–20.) For such a man acts in and from the ever-present heavens, or the celestial plane of his being.

This will lead us to consider the relation of the internal to the external in nature and in man, and to a discussion of the question, Is it possible for one mind so to influence another mind as to change his bodily condition from disease to health?

It was the doctrine of Bishop Berkeley that all the objects of nature of which we take cognizance by our sense-perceptions, are in their inmost reality only *ideas* in the mind. This was also the teaching of Plato, and is a fundamental tenet of the idealistic philosophy. All external things represent and express things in the mind. These ideas of things were supposed by Berkeley to be imprinted on our minds by the infinite Spirit in whom we live, and are moved, and have our being. He says: " The ideas imprinted on the senses by the Author of nature, are called real things; and those excited in the imagination being less regular, vivid, and constant, are more properly termed *ideas*, or *images* of *things*, which they copy and represent. But then our sensations, be they never so vivid and distinct, are nevertheless ideas, that is, they exist in the mind, or are perceived by it, as truly as the ideas of its own forming. The ideas of sense are allowed to have more reality in them, that is, to be more strong, orderly, and coherent, than the creatures of the mind; but this is no argument that they exist without the mind. They are also less dependent on the spirit, or thinking substance that perceives them, in that they are excited by the will of another and more powerful Spirit; yet still they are *ideas*, and certainly no idea, whether faint or strong, can exist otherwise than in a mind perceiving it." (*Treatise concerning the Principles of Human Knowledge*, sec. 30.)

Thus, what we call an external world is perpetually created in our minds, and is but the external or sensuous expression of ideas which we derive from the Infinite Mind. It is the projecting outward into the conditions of space and time of subjective conceptions. The science of the correspondence of external to internal things becomes an exact science, like geometry, when we learn the spiritual meaning of the objects of nature, or come to understand what idea or state of the mind each thing represents, and from which it arises into existence in us. What is true of the world at large is also true of the human body in its relation to the mind. Man, as the ancient sages taught, is a microcosm, and comprises in himself all that *appears* to be without. He is an epitome of the universe, as each drop is of the ocean. As in exhibitions of the stereopticon the images which appear upon the screen are only representations of things in the camera, so the external world, including the human body, is only a projection and shadow of an internal and real world. The inner is the substantial, the outer is the phenomenal. Change the internal picture or idea in the mind, as in the stereoptical camera, and you necessitate a modification of the external representation. If the mental image is that of disease or sorrow, if this is thrown upon the material and corporeal screen, it becomes a magnified representation of it in the body. Change this for the illuminated and transparent picture (or idea) of health and happiness, and it is projected into a physical expression. The *without* is always as the *within*, and the twain are one like cause and effect.

Admitting this theory of creation to be true — and it is inherently and intuitively rational — the inquiry arises, Can one finite mind excite in another mind ideas that shall have all the vividness of reality? Has the human mind, in a mitigated sense, a creative potentiality? Can it cause the appearance and the disappearance of the objects of sense? Professor Zöllner, of the University of Leipzig, admits that such a thing is possible, and introduces the fact to explain certain otherwise inexplicable phenomena witnessed in his experiments with Slade, such as the disappearance and subsequent reappearance of a table from the room. It was the evanescence from the mind, and the return to the mind of the *idea* of the table. When Jesus vanished from the sight of men, as he sometimes did, — which is also said to have been done by Apollonius of Tyana, — it was only the obliteration of his idea from men's minds. Is it possible thus to cause the evanescence of the thought and sensational image of disease from the mind of a patient? And can we create in him so vivid an idea of health, or of a certain bodily condition, that it shall be to him an absolute reality and actuality? We unhesitatingly answer in the affirmative. *It has been done, and consequently can be done again.* In the language of another, "That which we have heard, that which we have seen with our eyes, that which we beheld, and our hands handled, concerning the Word of life, declare we unto you." (1 John i : 1–3.)

Says Professor Zöllner: "We know from internal experience that our will is able up to a certain degree, by means of the so-called force of the imagination, to produce at pleasure representations of objects of sight *in our own soul*. In this case we recognize our *own* will as the cause of the representations. If, now, experiments could be instituted, in which this individual will (or imagination) of one man could produce in like manner, at pleasure, representative images in the soul of another, spatially separated from the willing agent, these images being clothed with all the attributes of reality which we ascribe to the so-called real or actual world surrounding us, thereby would experimental proof be afforded that the phenomenon of a *real, external world* can be produced and evoked by an individual will, joined with intelligence, in another individual.

"There remains only the question whether it is experimentally demonstrable that the human will (or imagination) is able to induce such vivid representations in the consciousness of another, that the latter regards them altogether as he regards the representations whose causes we ordinarily designate as *real objects or bodies*. Experiments of this kind have, in fact, been publicly instituted in Germany by the magnetizer, Hansen, of such a surprising and convincing nature that it is impossible to doubt the reality of the influence of an individual will upon another individual." (*Transcendental Physics*, pp. 150, 151.)

Experiments have also been made in France recently by M. Focachon, which conclusively prove the influence of one mind upon another mind, and through this medium upon the body, in the generation and cure of diseased conditions. Intelligent men and women in every part of the world are becoming aroused to the study of the occult powers of the human spirit, and to the investigation of the latent energies of the mind of man. The religious metaphysical philosophy of the East is becoming united to the practical science of Europe and America, and a higher development of man will be the result. The dormant, slumbering energies of the human soul will be awakened again into life and activity. A dead Christianity, which is only the petrifaction of the primitive system, and a still more defunct Buddhism, will be resuscitated and resume their youthful vigor. What are now accounted marvels of healing will become only ordinary events, like the morning succeeding the night, and spring following winter in regular succession.

If ideas are the inmost essence and reality of what we call external things, and God creates the world and all it contains of beauty and grandeur, by imprinting upon our minds the *ideas* of things, it is not an unreasonable supposition that man, who is made in the image and likeness of God, under certain conditions and limitations, may have a creative power and influence over the mind of another. The world exists subjectively, or in mind, before it is an objective reality. The same is true of the body of man. Why should it be thought a thing incredible that our influence over the mind of a passive subject may be sufficient to affect his bodily condition. The world is to us what we make it, and so is our physical organism. Our ideas and thoughts may be so transferred to the mind of a patient as to become his own. In the modern science of medicine, the blood of a healthy person is sometimes transferred to the veins of an invalid. But a transfusion of our mental life into another is a thousand times better. This is the divine method, and is what Jesus did. The injunction of Paul has here a special application, "Be ye imitators of God, as beloved children." (Eph. v : 1.) These old and forgotten truths will again be re-established and as conclusively proved as are any of the principles of chemistry, and out of them will arise the divinest and most efficient system of healing the souls and bodies of men the world has ever seen. In the principle we have illustrated above, we are getting down to the bottom fact and underlying reality in the cures effected by Jesus the Christ. He had power to vanish from the sight of men, by expunging from their minds the sensational image of himself, and he possessed the ability to obliterate from the minds of the sick the idea of their malady, and to imprint upon their receptive souls the idea of health and wholeness. During the eighteen centuries which have elapsed since his material manifestation he has lost none of his power to save (or heal). For in the realm of spirit, into which his living consciousness has been translated, he is "the same yesterday, to-day, and forever." What he ever accomplished, he can do now, and can so impart his life as the risen and ascended Christ to men, that they may do the same. In the lapse of humanity in its organic unity (which is called Adam) from the high table-land of the spiritual and celestial into the sensuous and fleshly range of the mind, the deific powers of human nature became dormant; but they are not dead. Man in the descending scale of life has touched the bottom, and is rebounding upward. In the restoration of the spiritual life of humanity will come back the power " to work the works of God." When we come to view man, not as a material body, but as a " living soul," which is never sundered from the Infinite Mind, we shall recover our lost dominion over the works of God, especially our own body.

The fundamental principle in the practice of the phrenopathic method of cure is the recognition of the true idea of man as already in his true being an immortal spirit, and as such, exempt from sin and disease. In our conception of the patient we divest him of the material and astral envelope, and think of him not as about to be saved in some future time, but as *already saved*, so far as his true being is concerned. We, as it were, *dematerialize* him in our idea of him. Through the influence of mind upon mind, and in accordance with the law of thought-transference, this serves to dispossess him of the idea and belief of disease, and free him from his engrossment by the illusions of sense. It may be objected to such a method of mental cure, that it is too transcendental, and but a few are sufficiently unfolded spiritually to practise it with any degree of success. In reply we would only say that the intelligent force which creates and governs the world is transcendental; that is, it is purely mental and is beyond the grasp of the senses, but is none the less real and potential for all that. It is quite true that only a comparatively small number of persons are at present qualified to practice the system with marked success. But it has been our aim to educate men and women up to that degree of spiritual development that will greatly increase the number of successful practitioners. It may, in truth, be said of surgery, that only a small fraction of the twelve hundred millions of the human race are qualified to be eminently skillful surgeons. Yet that is no weighty objection to the modern science of surgery which is accomplishing such marvels in saving life. The good surgeon, like the poet, is born, not made. The same is true of the phrenopathic healer.

The system of cure that has been advocated and its principles expounded in these pages, and in the volumes which have preceded this, is fundamentally at variance with the dominant scientific materialism of the day. It has been the fashion for some centuries to believe and teach that it is *the body which* makes the mind; that the soul is a function of the organism, or of some part of it, as, for instance, the brain, and is entirely dependent upon and governed by the organism. This is coming to be viewed by many as a total inversion of the truth, as a moustrous perversion of the true idea of man, and a degrading doctrine against which there is a manifest reaction and revolt in the public mind. In every age of human history, and in all nationalities, there have been philosophers who have held that the soul makes and governs the body. But in our European and Western civilizations, owing to the prevalence of materialism, the teaching of such men has been a voice crying in the wilderness, with few to hear. The idealists, who have ever constituted the more spiritual portion of mankind, affirm that the external form and condition of man are dependent upon his internal state; that it is the nature of mind, or spirit, to ultimate itself in a bodily expression in harmony with it. The habitual indulgence of certain evil passions alters the conformation of the face and the whole body, and the man, in accordance with a divine law, becomes externally what he is internally, so far as such a change can be effected in one brief life on earth. The man who yields to the indulgence of the animal and selfish appetites and propensities, begins to *look* animal and selfish. The habitual belief of those false and illusive ideas which constitute mental disease, those *opinions* which prevail in the world, which become a prominent part of our education, but which are without foundation in truth, will sooner or later ultimate themselves in physical maladies. For it is an established law of divine order that a man must inevitably in time become outwardly what he is inwardly, and in this life physically what he is mentally. Our system of mental cure recognizes and emphasizes this universal principle. We seek in harmony with it to commence the cure of disease from within, to inaugurate a change in the mental *status* of a patient, which must with undeviating certainty translate itself into a corporeal expression. We aim to prepare the man, not only for the life that is, but also for all the life which is to come. It is a prominent intent of the current religious instruction of the day to prepare men to die. That string has been harped upon until it is well-nigh worn out. The philosophy which we advocate aims to prepare men never to die, to view death as an illusion, and to lead the disciple to the attainment of that knowledge of God, and our relation to him, which is eternal life. We enter the sick-room, not to confer upon the patient the useless sacrament of extreme unction to fit him to die, and to smooth his passage into purgatory, but to light in the consciousness of the sufferer the quenchless torch of a present immortality, and faith in a present and full salvation, and to close the gates of Hades against his ingress into its dark domains. All the virtues of life and truths of faith, which are the formative principles of a celestial and angelic character, are recommended. As one has well said, "A man of pure and angelic character begins inevitably to present a pure and angelic appearance; the countenance becomes placid, the manner sedate; and the soul of man transforms his body until it becomes as angelic as is compatible with its present relations: and when it assumes a new form after what is called death, what shall prevent it from assuming the one most appropriate to its nature?" (*The Blazing Star*, by William B. Green, p. 166.)

It has been our aim, in what we have said in this volume, to restore Christianity to something of its original meaning in the religious consciousness of men; to winnow away the accumulated and useless chaff, and preserve the divine and living seed; to divest it of all that is non-essential to it, and which can only be viewed by the enlightened minds of to-day as a subsequent disfiguring addition to the primitive system. We have endeavored to transport our mind back through the centuries and come face to face with the incarnated Christ, and reverently listen to the words of him who spake as never man before spake. In giving an esoteric, or inside, view of Christianity as a system of saving and healing truth, we have, of course, failed to do full justice to the subject. No artist ever yet succeeded in painting the rainbow that spans the eastern heavens after a storm. He only does the best he can, and we add to what he does his evident good intention, and accept the picture as an aid to recalling in our own minds the true and perfect idea of the bow of promise which God has placed upon the clouds. Christianity is inseparable from the living personality of Jesus the Christ. None but he can fully expound it and reveal it. If our attempt to do so shall bring any one to sit at his feet and listen to him as he still inly speaks to men, we shall not have written in vain. The system of mental healing must ever be kept within the domain of a genuine Christianity. Outside of the system of truth taught the world by Jesus, it will be as powerless to save as was the staff of Elijah, separated from the hands of the prophet and in the grasp of his servant, to raise to life the dead son of the Shunamite woman. The fundamental idea of Christianity as a system of salvation, as also of the mental-cure system of to-day, is that the Christ is the supreme living principle, and the Christ-life in us is the only real and immortal life. All other life is mutable and evanescent. He is a Christian in the full-orbed meaning of that word in whom there is a reincarnation of the intellectual and moral life of Jesus. "He who lives the life shall *know* of the doctrine." It is only by doing the truth that it becomes so incorporated into our inner being as to become a part of our living self. Then it is not an external garment to be put on and off as occasion may require, but "the life of God in the soul of man." The inner self, when it is composed of the truths of faith, as the external body is of the elements of the world, is as immortal as are those truths. The fully instructed soul is but the formulation into a living personality of God's truth. "Mark the perfect man (the fully initiated) and behold the upright (the spiritually enlightened), for the end of that man is peace," which is the opposite of mental disease. (Ps. xxxvii: 37.) He in whom the Christ dwells and acts is invested with the silent omnipotence of truth, and will be a saving power in the age in which he lives. In all such as have fellowship (or community of life) with Jesus he multiplies and spiritually propagates himself, and the Christ, as the manifested God, becomes more and more incarnated in humanity. In the language of the leader of the Brahmo Somaj, or Church of God, in India, "The Spirit-Christ spreads thus forth in the universe as an emanation from the Divine Reason, and you can see him with the eye of faith underlying all the endless varieties of truth and goodness in ancient and modern times. He is the Christ as the principle of pure spiritual intelligence, the Word of God, mighty Logos. Scattered in all men and women of the East and the West are multitudinous Christ-principles and fragments of Christ-life, one vast and identical Sonship diversely manifested." It is our sincere prayer that the mental-cure movement, now growing into such proportions in Europe and America, may be a tributary stream to swell the vast current of the Christ-life in the world, until the earth shall be full of the saving knowledge of God as the waters cover the deep.

CONQUER AND REST.

"Why not learn to conquer sorrow?
    Why not learn to smile at pain?
Why should every stormy morrow
    Shroud our way in gloom again?

"Why not lift the soul immortal
    Up to its angelic height —
Bid it pass the radiant portal
    Of the world of faith and light?

"Oh! there is another being
    All about us, all above,
Hid from mortal sense or seeing,
    Save the nameless sense of love.

"Not the love that dies like roses,
    When the frost-fire scathes the sod,
But the eternal rest that closes
    Round the soul that dwells in God.

"Into this great habitation
    Never tear or sorrow came;
Oh! it is the new creation,
    God its light, and love its flame.

"Up, O soul! and dwell forever
    On this hidden, glorious shore;
Chilled by cloud-shade, never, never;
    Up, and dwell for evermore."

www.ingramcontent.com/pod-product-compliance
Lightning Source LLC
Chambersburg PA
CBHW032227080426
42735CB00008B/745